AMY-JILL LEVINE

ENTERING THE PASSION *of* JESUS

A BEGINNER'S GUIDE to HOLY WEEK

Abingdon Press
Nashville

ENTERING THE PASSION OF JESUS
A BEGINNER'S GUIDE TO HOLY WEEK

Library of Congress Cataloging-in-Publication has been requested.

978-1-5018-6955-6

18 19 20 21 22 23 24 25 26 27 — 10 9 8 7 6 5 4 3 2 1
MANUFACTURED IN THE UNITED STATES OF AMERICA

To the churches, synods, presbyteries, diocese,
and other Christian groups that have welcomed me,
in gratitude for your hospitality.

CONTENTS

INTRODUCTION

The Passion accounts in all four Gospels speak to my heart. They are stories of failure and courage, despair and hope, political machinations and theological inspiration. I want all readers of the Gospels to read the Passion stories with *com*passion: to see how much more meaningful they become when we learn the history behind the texts and study the texts themselves to see what brilliant writers the Evangelists were.

This is not your ordinary Lenten study. In the chapters that follow, we delve into the history and literature of the last days of Jesus' life. We find ways to understand and question our own lives through the stories of his trials and choices. This Lenten journey challenges us to examine our consciences and find out how deepening our relationship with Jesus and the Bible brings us into closer relationship with others and the world.

In every good story, there is history and there is risk; and the stories of Holy Week, also called Passion Week, are brimming with both history and risk. The history provides the foundation and often explains what's going on and why. If we get the history

wrong, we will misunderstand what the Gospel writers are trying
to tell us. The risk brings the anticipation, the danger, and the
potential for great loss or great reward. We should always be
willing to take a risk when we do a Bible study, for any Bible study
should open up new readings and new ideas. We should not read
the text, or understand the Passion narrative, the same way we
did when we were children. New information about the history
may cause us to rethink previously held views; new insights into
the Gospel text may even cause us to rethink how we act in the
world today.

And yet, there is also deep stability in the stories. Nothing in
the doing of history or the study of the literature can ever take
away from the theological claims of the church. There is nothing
in these lessons that compromises the creeds you may proclaim
or the deep beliefs you hold. Investigations into history and the
study of the Gospels as narratives should serve to enhance and
enrich one's faith.

In this study, we explore both the history behind the stories
of Holy Week and the risks taken not only by Jesus but also by
his followers. But this study is not only a review of Jesus' Passion.
It's also a form of personal introspection. Jesus is about to give up
his life, which requires determining what a life is worth. And that
means we all have to determine what our own lives are worth.
What is worth dying for? What is worth living for? What are our
values, and have we lived up to them?

Lent is also a period of atonement, which is a time to repair
past wrongs. We might think of the term "atonement" as meaning
"at one-ment," being at one with one another, being reconciled.
One way of understanding the cross is that it represents
atonement between humanity and divinity, in that Jesus takes the
responsibility for the sins of human beings and cancels them out

with his death. But the Passion narrative should also prompt us to think about reconciliation in our own lives.

During Lent, we should ask ourselves, what should I have done that I did not do? What risk should I have taken that I was afraid to take? When did my sense of self-preservation trump my sense of courage? Jesus not only takes up his own cross, Mark 8:34 states, "He called the crowd with his disciples, and said to them, 'If any want to become my followers, let them deny themselves and take up their cross and follow me.'" Matthew 10:38 repeats the point: "and whoever does not take up the cross and follow me is not worthy of me." The Passion narrative asks much of us, and it also, through Jesus' example, gives us the knowledge that we can do what we are asked, and the assurance that we will succeed.

The Passion narrative asks much of us, and it also, through Jesus' example, gives us the knowledge that we can do what we are asked, and the assurance that we will succeed.

The gospel is not always easy to follow. Jesus talks about the narrow gate: "For the gate is narrow and the road is hard that leads to life, and there are few who find it" (Matthew 7:14). He doesn't say that being a disciple is going to be a walk in the park. Passing through the narrow gate means putting ourselves at risk. It means asking, what should I have done, even if it might have been detrimental to me? It means asking, what did I do that I should not have done, and how might I correct the results? Entering into Lent is the time when we ask those questions, and we then take the next step and answer them.

Holy Week is a time to think about risk, because that's what this whole Passion narrative represents. We watch those around Jesus—his disciples, his friends, his companions who have been with him since those early days of the ministry in Galilee. These are the companions who watched him heal the sick, feed the multitudes, and proclaim the good news. Yet we see them now, in that fateful last week, betraying him, denying him, running away from him. These are stories not only of Judas and Peter, of John and James; they are our stories as well. Who stands firm and who runs? What happens when you run? And what can we do, now that we have failed ourselves and others, to find that "at one-ment" again? Whom do we need to bring back, and who will bring us back? We know it is possible to find this reconciliation, because the God of grace makes it possible.

These are the kinds of things we should be thinking about as we enter Holy Week. What does it mean to misunderstand, to fail? What does it mean to deny, to betray, or to fall asleep when we should have acted? And then how do we rise again? I think the story is meant to move us emotionally, in terms of conscience, to indict and to challenge. And it is meant to move us ethically, from faith into action. If we can accept the risk, we can become better people.

This story, the Passion narrative, works on me. The literature is just that powerful. How do I know that it is that powerful? I know because even though I am not a Christian, I can recognize its power. I can feel it move me, every time I read it, in all four Gospels in which it appears. And I have seen it work, over and over again, in my Christian friends, my students, and churches worldwide.

I come to you as a Jewish person who is deeply familiar with the New Testament, and with how Christians have understood it over the centuries. I also come to you as a historian who has spent her entire career studying the New Testament both in its historical context and its multiple interpretations over time. My job at Vanderbilt University is to help candidates for Christian ministry understand the text that grounds their vocation and guides their lives.

To study Jesus and the Gospels is in fact to study Jewish history: Jesus was a Jew as were all his early followers. In studying the New Testament, I am therefore studying the Jewish history that I never learned in my own synagogue.

What can a Jewish person teach you about the Gospels? I would not have spent my life studying the New Testament if I did not think the subject worthwhile and even inspirational. Although I do not worship Jesus, I find much of his message of the kingdom of heaven compelling. In the numerous church-based programs I have done, almost unfailingly someone asks me, "A.-J., you've read the New Testament numerous times, and it's clear you have a deep appreciation for the teaching of Jesus of Nazareth. So, why aren't you a Christian?" It's a fair question. Here is how I respond: Belief, or faith, is a matter not of logic, or of academic ability. It is a matter of grace and so a matter of calling, of vocation. I am, personally, completely fulfilled in my own tradition, and yet—and yet—I see the beauty and the wonder in the gospel story. I can, as a historian, guide my students to read more closely, to find more meaning, and to appreciate more deeply this magnificent text. And if I as a Jew can see so much profound teaching in these pages, surely my Christian friends can find even more. I do not seek to challenge Christian theological claims. Instead, I seek, through my studies and my teaching, to enhance them.

In a sense, Lent, and especially Holy Week, is a lot like the ten days leading up to the Jewish holiday of Yom Kippur.

Those days, between Rosh HaShanah, the new year, and Yom Kippur, the Day of Atonement, represent a time of introspection during which Jewish people take stock of what we have done, what we did not do well, and what we failed to do. We assess our relationships with others—family, friends, neighbors, and even the people we do not like. We take time to repair broken relationships. We realize that we may have hurt someone, and we take the time to apologize.

These ten days between Rosh HaShanah and Yom Kippur are called the Days of Awe. At the culmination of those days comes Yom Kippur, the Day of Atonement. On that day, Jewish people fast and pray, and we make sure we have addressed whatever it is we should have taken care of. The tradition is that we go up to someone whom we have hurt or we think we might have hurt, and we say, "I'm really sorry I've said this." Or even harder, "I'm sorry I didn't step up and support you. I'm sorry that when you asked me to come help you do something, I said I was busy. I really should have helped you." Or, "I'm really sorry I didn't visit you in the hospital. I should have been there."

This type of reconciliation is what Jesus is talking about in the Sermon on the Mount, when he states, "So when you are offering your gift at the altar, if you remember that your brother or sister has something against you, leave your gift there before the altar and go; first be reconciled to your brother or sister, and then come and offer your gift" (Matthew 5:23-24). Before we come to church, sing the hymns, and offer our gifts, we should be reconciled to our friends, our neighbors, and, yes, even our enemies. Again, such work is not easy, but it is both possible and necessary.

More, saying "sorry" is not enough. We must move from regret and remorse to correction and to action. Just as Jesus at the Last Supper, proclaims, "This cup that is poured out for you is the new covenant in my blood" (Luke 22:20) and so sets up a new relationship, so we establish new relationships as well. His disciples commit not just to an apology, but to a life of service and of love.

The Days of Awe are ten days when we think: How could I have been a better *me*? How could we, as a community, have been a better *us*? What do we need to do to move forward so that the next year will be better than the year before?

It is through this lens of atonement and reconciliation that I understand both Lent and the Passion narrative. There's a tradition in Judaism that says the Book of Life is open on Rosh HaShanah and it is sealed on Yom Kippur. When the book is open, we pray that God will write us in for a good year as opposed to a not-so-good year. The Rosh HaShanah greeting is

During Lent
you have the opportunity to think about your life alongside the life of Jesus, inviting inward transformation and then outward action.

"l'shanah tovah tikatevu ve techatemu," or, "may you be inscribed and sealed for a good year [in the Book of Life]." There is a sense of getting the books straight. Similarly, during Lent you have the opportunity to think about your life alongside the life of Jesus, inviting inward transformation and then outward action.

We can see the same imagery of the Book of Life in the New Testament. The Book of Revelation uses the term "book of life" frequently, as in Revelation 20:12, "And I saw the dead, great and small, standing before the throne, and books were opened. Also another book was opened, the book of life. And the dead were judged according to their works, as recorded in the books." Even Paul uses this expression in Philippians 4:3, "Yes, and I ask you also, my loyal companion, help these women [Euodia and Syntyche, two leaders of the community who are in disagreement], for they have struggled beside me in the work of the gospel, together with Clement and the rest of my co-workers, whose names are in the book of life."

Lent is a season of the liturgical year where for forty days (not counting Sundays), Christians talk about Jesus' journey to the cross. The stories told are not about the happy, glory days in Galilee where Jesus is feeding five thousand or raising the dead. These stories are about the inexorable move to suffering and death. We know what's about to happen, and there's nothing we can do to stop it. Jesus announced his Passion clearly, three times in the Gospels. His followers didn't believe him. We don't want to believe him either. We do not want to see our friend hanging on a cross. Despite the fact that we know there's a resurrection at the end, we still have to go through the horror before we can get to the healing. Lent becomes then an opportunity for us to become reflective. We're facing death, so what should we have done that we didn't do?

Lent also tells us that Jesus had a choice. He did not

But he makes the right choice, the hard choice: "Yet not what I want but what you want" (Matthew 26:39). And so he asks his followers to choose, to make the right choices, even if they are difficult.

have to go up to Jerusalem, where he knew he would die. He did not have to accept the cup assigned to him, and he does not want to suffer. As he so poignantly prays in Gethsemane, "My Father, if it is possible, let this cup pass from me." But he makes the right choice, the hard choice: "Yet not what I want but what you want" (Matthew 26:39). And so he asks his followers to choose, to make the right choices, even if they are difficult.

As we have noted, Sundays in Lent are not counted as part of the forty days. Each Sunday in Lent is also an anticipation of, a reminder of, Easter Sunday. That is a day of joy. Thus, the season of Lent also gives Jesus' followers a time for rejoicing: there is always good news; there is a future that can be, that will be, better. We can read the story retrospectively, because we know the ending. The time is still open. The mission is ongoing. God is merciful.

The six chapters that follow journey through Jesus' last days from the Triumphal Entry into Jerusalem to his prayerful agony in Gethsemane. They are stories of risk. Jesus risks arrest when he enters Jerusalem to public acclaim and so brings himself to the attention of those who see his kingship as a challenge to their own political authority. He turns over tables at the Temple, and thus risks the results of righteous anger. His risks continue as he then teaches in the Temple and faces challenges to his proclamation.

He is not alone in this risky business. His disciples knew the risks: they have associated themselves with a man who has made enemies of the high priests; they are friends with a man whom Pontius Pilate, the Roman governor, sees as a threat. They are followers of a man who will be crucified as an enemy of the Roman State, and as a "king."

The woman who anoints him takes a risk—not only of public criticism for her act of love and generosity. She risks even whether

Jesus will accept her gift of generosity. And he does. The women who come to the tomb to anoint his body take risks, for they seek to minister to a man put to death by Roman capital punishment. One takes a risk when one says, "I am a follower of Jesus"; one takes a greater risk by *acting* on that identification.

Many years ago, when my children were quite young, Vanderbilt divinity students would sometimes babysit them when my husband and I had an evening meeting (or, when we just needed to go out to dinner by ourselves). At times, the children's two favorite babysitters were unable to come because of their field education placements. They may have been on a mission trip, or they were working at Nashville's "Room In The Inn" program. My children said, "They can't come because they are being Christian." My husband and I thought that was a splendid definition of the term "Christian."

Jesus calls on the scriptural history of sacrifice and sacrificial meals as he eats with the disciples at the Last Supper and presents them with his body and blood. He risks misunderstanding, for his disciples cannot accept the fact that he must die, despite his several predictions of his Passion. One risks participating in this meal today, however it is named or practiced (Holy Communion, Eucharist, the Lord's Supper, Fellowship meal, and so on). To break bread with someone is to signal fellowship and more: It indicates membership in the same family. It means including those who may have felt, or may have been, excluded.

Finally, in Gethsemane Jesus is abandoned by those closest to him. Three disciples fall asleep; another disciple betrays him; Mark 14:50 tells us, "All of them deserted him and fled." Jesus prays for the cup to pass, and we are reminded of the cup that "runneth over" in Psalm 23:5 (KJV), and the cup that Jesus has just lifted to his disciples at the Last Supper. History and symbols and opportunities for risk course through the events of Holy Week, and we are called to place ourselves with Jesus, from the Triumphal Entry to the Temple to the two suppers, and on to Gethsemane and then the cross.

This study and the story of Jesus' last days bring with them several challenges: What do we stand for? What do we believe in? When do we stand up for those beliefs? We can also watch the disciples and ask ourselves, when have we denied or betrayed? How can we make it right? Jesus talks about taking up the cross. The Passion narrative shows him doing that. Can those who claim to be his followers do the same?

When a friend comes to you and says, "What is the cross that you're bearing? What is the cause that you have taken up? How much have you risked?," do you know what your answer is? That's entering into Lent. That's entering the Passion.

Chapter 1

Jerusalem: Risking Reputation

Chapter 1

JERUSALEM: RISKING REPUTATION

When they had come near Jerusalem and had reached Bethphage, at the Mount of Olives, Jesus sent two disciples, saying to them, "Go into the village ahead of you, and immediately you will find a donkey tied, and a colt with her; untie them and bring them to me. If anyone says anything to you, just say this, 'The Lord needs them.' And he will send them immediately." This took place to fulfill what had been spoken through the prophet, saying,

> *"Tell the daughter of Zion,*
> *Look, your king is coming to you,*
> *humble, and mounted on a donkey,*
> *and on a colt, the foal of a donkey."*

*The disciples went and did as Jesus had directed
them; they brought the donkey and the colt, and
put their cloaks on them, and he sat on them. A
very large crowd spread their cloaks on the road,
and others cut branches from the trees and spread
them on the road. The crowds that went ahead of
him and that followed were shouting,*

> *"Hosanna to the Son of David!*
> *Blessed is the one who comes in the name*
> *of the Lord!*
> *Hosanna in the highest heaven!"*

*When he entered Jerusalem, the whole city was in
turmoil, asking, "Who is this?" The crowds were
saying, "This is the prophet Jesus from Nazareth
in Galilee."*

Matthew 21:1-11

The Gospels give us four versions of Jesus' entry into
Jerusalem: Matthew 21:1-11; Mark 11:1-11; Luke 19:28-44; and
John 12:12-19. Each has a different emphasis; each has specific
details that contribute to the greater whole. No one Gospel can
tell the full story, and each should be savored for the story it tells.
In this chapter, we concentrate on Matthew's version, remarking
throughout on the distinctive elements in the other versions.
Each Gospel deserves its own full treatment, so ideally you will
read the other accounts on your own, closely, to compare what
message each seeks to convey.

In the story of Jesus' triumphal entry, there are prophecies
and characters from the Scriptures of Israel—what the church
calls the "Old Testament" and what Jews call the "Tanakh"

(an acronym for Torah [Instruction], Nevi'im [Prophets], and Ketuvim [Writings])—that provide the color and explanation for what's going on—the donkey and the colt, the humble savior, the cries of "Hosanna!," even the palms. For Jesus, the risk of riding into Jerusalem in a victory parade is very real. Pontius Pilate is also making an appearance as he comes, with his entourage, into Jerusalem to tell the Jewish people celebrating the Passover, the "Feast of Freedom" from slavery and oppression, that Rome is in charge. And Jesus' entry calls attention to himself in a major way. Tensions are running high, as are expectations: of liberation, of freedom, of autonomy. As Jesus enters into town on a donkey with the crowd crying out for him, the Passion begins.

Tensions are running high, as are expectations: of liberation, of freedom, of autonomy. As Jesus enters into town on a donkey with the crowd crying out for him, the Passion begins.

The triumphal entry of Jesus into Jerusalem, celebrated on Palm Sunday, is the start of Passion Week. It also begins a story of tragedy and triumph that should inspire, provoke, and challenge. We who are familiar with the New Testament—or who have seen one of the numerous "Jesus" movies popular during Lent—know how the story goes: in less than a week after this grand entry parade, the crowds are calling for Jesus' death.

We know what will happen, for Jesus had already three times told his followers of his fate. He has taught them "that the Son of Man must undergo great suffering, and be rejected by the elders, the chief priests, and the scribes, and be killed, and after three days rise again." He wasn't teaching in parables or using metaphors. Mark insists, "He said all this quite openly" (Mark 8:31-32a).

We also know that this story, this Triumphal Entry, will have a happy ending. Jesus had several times announced to his disciples that the cross was not the end of the story, that betrayal can be overcome, that justice does prevail, and that sacrifice can lead to redemption. He proclaims resurrection, something in which most Jews believed and which some Jews to this day, including in my own Orthodox synagogue, still proclaim. According to Jewish liturgy, God is to be praised for "giving life to the dead."

To be sure, good stories deserve repeating, and good lessons warrant reiteration. And yet we can do more. Let's start with Matthew's story, a story that should not only inspire, it should surprise; it should not only challenge, it should also delight. It is a good story in which the narrative art of the Gospel writer perfectly matches the profound theology that the story seeks to convey.

The Meek King

Let's watch again: We're on the outskirts of Jerusalem, the city that was holy then as it is holy now to the Jewish community. It is the capital of Judea, and it is the site of the Temple to which Jews would already be coming as pilgrims at Passover. The city would swell with Jews celebrating the Feast of Freedom, the end of slavery, the exodus from Egypt, the time of redemption. Thousands upon thousands would come to Jerusalem—from Athens and Egypt, Babylon and Rome, Damascus, and, of course, Galilee.

But then something quite strange happens.

Jesus tells two of his followers: "Go into the village ahead of you, and immediately you will find a donkey tied, and a colt with her; untie them and bring them to me. If anyone says anything to you, just say this, 'The Lord needs them.' And he will send them immediately" (Matthew 21:2-3).

Imagine this in our context: A popular leader sends two members of his entourage from, say, a respectable suburb into the downtown area of a big city, with the instructions, "You will find a Lexus sedan, and next to it a sports car—bring them to me. And if anyone asks, 'Hey, what are you doing with those cars?,' just say, 'The Lord needs them.' That'll be fine." Not likely! The next call will not be for spiritual redemption; it will be to 911 to report two stolen cars.

Matthew could be saying that Jesus had supernatural powers that not only allowed him to know where a donkey and colt could be found but also granted him the charisma such that his disciples could simply take what they wanted. I find it more likely that Jesus had friends in the area—especially if the colt is located in or near Bethany, two miles from Jerusalem, where his friends Mary, Martha, and Lazarus live.

The Gospel of John tells us that Jesus had been to Jerusalem several times. Right after the sign of turning water into wine at the wedding in Cana, "the Passover of the Jews was near, and Jesus went up to Jerusalem" (John 2:13). He surely found followers there, for "when he was in Jerusalem during the Passover festival, many believed in his name because they saw the signs that he was doing" (John 2:23). In John 5:1, again we read, "There was a festival of the Jews, and Jesus went up to Jerusalem." John does not name what festival this is, but the most likely feast here would be what Jews call "Shavuot," the "Feast of Weeks"; the holiday that celebrates the giving of the Torah to Moses on Mount Sinai, is known in Greek as "Pentecost." For the church, it is at Pentecost when, according to Acts 2, the Holy Spirit descends on the apostles. For Jews, Shavuot marks the time, fifty days after the exodus from Egypt, when Moses received the Torah at Mount Sinai and gave it to the people Israel. In John 10:22, we are told that Jesus again went up to Jerusalem for the "festival of the Dedication." That title refers to the holiday of Hanukkah, when the Jewish people regained their independence from the Syrian-Greeks who in the second century BCE had attempted to prevent them from following their own religious beliefs and practices. (Interestingly, the first recording of this event is in the books of 1 and 2 Maccabees, which are part of the canon of some Christian groups. Christians kept the history; Jews have the holiday.) Jesus is familiar with Jerusalem, and the people in the city know him, or at least they think they do.

Let's stop to consider the geographical symbolism that begins the Passion narrative. Jerusalem is the Holy City, but it is also occupied by the Romans. When we enter into a place where we know we oppose the local leaders, what do we do? What do we say? How do we plan ahead?

Jesus most likely planned this entry; the symbolism is no less significant even if it had been carefully staged. If one is going to confront any system that prevents human wholeness—be it poverty, sickness, colonialism, or lack of compassion—it helps to have a plan.

Jesus' plans extended beyond a particular concern for transportation. According to Matthew, the obtaining of the donkey "took place to fulfill what had been spoken through the prophet, saying, 'Tell the daughter of Zion, Look, your king is coming to you, humble, and mounted on a donkey, and on a colt, the foal of a donkey'" (Matthew 21:4-5).*

Again, we should stop and savor what Matthew is doing.

---

* The citation is a combination of Zechariah 9:9 and Isaiah 62:11.

When a Gospel text cites the Scriptures of Israel—and Matthew does this frequently—our readings are enhanced when we look at the full context of those citations. Zechariah 9:9 is surrounded by verses that confirm and enrich the single verse. In Zechariah 9:11, the prophet proclaims, "because of the blood of my covenant with you, I will set your prisoners free from the waterless pit." Thus, Matthew is cluing us in: not only is the time of redemption coming, it is coming with the assurance that God is faithful to the covenants. The Triumphal Entry anticipates the Last Supper.

If we look at Zechariah's full prophecy, we see even more relevant material. Zechariah 9:9, which has six lines, also proclaims, "Lo, your king comes to you; / triumphant and victorious is he." The word the NRSV translates as "triumphant" really means, in Hebrew, "righteous." The focus for Zechariah, and for Jesus, is not on militaristic conquering, but on the power of justice.

We should also pay attention to the nuances of the part of the verse Matthew records. When Zechariah, and then Matthew, describes the coming king as "humble," the term does not mean "meek" or "gentle." The Hebrew has the connotation of being "poor" or "afflicted." This king does not enter with the trappings of royalty or a military parade or a twenty-one-gun salute. That is not the type of rule he teaches. The Greek term that the NRSV translates as "meek" refers to someone in authority who does not lord it over others. Followers of Jesus may be familiar with Psalm 37:11, "But the meek shall inherit the earth; and shall delight themselves in the abundance of peace" (KJV). This is the verse to which Jesus alludes in the Beatitudes that open the Sermon on the Mount: "Blessed are the meek, for they will inherit the earth" (Matthew 5:5).

Inheriting the earth, for the psalm and for the Gospel, requires being humble, not in the sense of lowly, but in the sense of being able to listen to others, to share resources, to prioritize community rather than authority, to serve rather than to be served. All that underlies the words from Zechariah, and Matthew's first-century Jewish audience would have known it.

> **Inheriting the earth,** for the psalm and for the Gospel, requires being humble, not in the sense of lowly, but in the sense of being able to listen to others, to share resources, to prioritize community rather than authority, to serve rather than to be served.

According to the NRSV's translation of Zechariah 9:9, this entering king is "victorious." Again, the Hebrew offers a different nuance. The Hebrew term translated "victorious" literally means "saved." It comes from the same root as the term "hosanna" and the names Hosea, Joshua, and, yes, Jesus. The Greek of this term really means "savior." We find the same Hebrew word, together with a reference to a king, in Psalm 33:16, which reads, "A king is not saved by his great army; a warrior is not delivered by his great strength."

Finally, Matthew's citation also alludes to Isaiah 62:11, "Say to daughter Zion...." The prophet continues: "See, your salvation comes" and then describes the people whom daughter Zion represents: "They shall be called, 'The Holy People, The Redeemed of the LORD'" (Isaiah 62:12a).

Zechariah speaks of a king who does not lord it over others, but who takes his place with those who are suffering. Zechariah speaks of a king who is righteous rather than violent. Zechariah speaks about a king who is strong in faith, not armed to the teeth. Isaiah speaks of rejoicing, community, and redemption. Reading Zechariah 9:9 and Isaiah 62:11 in their full contexts adds much to this story. The more we know about the original texts, the richer our reading of the Gospels that cite them becomes.

The disciples obtain the donkey and the colt, and we readers, now informed about Matthew's citation, get the implications of all the words that are used. So far, so good. But then, there is another potential problem in this story, heard if we listen carefully. Matthew writes, "The disciples went and did as Jesus had directed them; they brought the donkey and the colt, and put their cloaks on them, and he sat on them" (Matthew 21:6-7). Right, Matthew says that Jesus sat "on *them*." At this point, numerous first-year New Testament students conclude that Jesus rode two animals at the same time. That would certainly cause people to take notice when he rode into town. The victory parade would have become a circus! It is more likely that the word *them* referred to the cloaks spread on the animals and not the animals themselves.

Why then does Matthew, and only Matthew, mention the two animals? Zechariah's quotation uses what is called "poetic parallelism," a popular form of Hebrew poetry in which the second line enhances the first. For example, in one of the Bible's oldest poems, the Song of Deborah, we find, "He asked water and she gave him milk, she brought him curds in a lordly bowl" (Judges 5:25). The point is not that Jael gave the enemy general Sisera both a glass of milk and some cottage cheese; the second stanza explains what sort of milk product he received. Similarly, Zechariah, poetically, is speaking of one animal. But Matthew takes the parallelism literally and includes two donkeys.

I imagine Matthew, writing this line and thinking, "Does Jesus fulfill prophecy?" and then answering, "You bet he does!"

Matthew reports that, as Jesus enters the city, a huge crowd "spread their cloaks on the road, and others cut branches from the trees and spread them on the road" (Matthew 21:8). Do we recognize what is missing here? The Triumphal Entry is most commonly associated with Palm Sunday, and so we expect in this scene to find the crowds waving their palm branches. But there is no mention of palms in Matthew, just a reference to branches. Only John's Gospel mentions the palms (12:13). Granted, this may seem like a trivial point: why should we care if the branches are palm or myrtle or willow? We should care because we should listen closely each time Scripture is read, lest we impose our own concerns—or palm branches—on it rather than allow ourselves to be challenged by the actual words of the story.

More, those missing palms can tell us something about ourselves. We see what we expect to see, and at times these expectations trip us up. We read what is not there, and, as a result, we fail to see what *is* there. But the whole message of the Bible, and specifically of the kingdom of heaven, is to see the world otherwise: as God wants it to be rather than as it is. That is why Jesus taught his followers to pray, "your kingdom come, your will be done." Along with reading the Gospels in light of one another and taking one detail from Matthew and another from John, we should also attend to the individual stories. That's why the church preserved four Gospels in the canon, not just one. No one Gospel tells the entire story; no one Gospel could. But each can give us different messages, and different images. And each should be savored.

We realize, very quickly, that each Gospel has its own story to tell. No one Gospel, no single account, can contain all of what the good news is. We should listen carefully to all four Gospels, and in recognizing their separate emphases, we can see how the story speaks to different, but all valid, concerns. We have already seen how Matthew, for example, is particularly invested in the relationship between Jesus and the Scriptures of Israel, those texts about which he insisted, "Do not think that I have come to abolish the law [that is, the Torah] or the prophets; I have come not to abolish but to fulfill" (Matthew 5:17). No wonder Matthew gives us so many citations to these ancient texts. Some of Matthew's original readers would have known them, and because they knew those earlier Scriptures, they heard the gospel with more finely attuned ears.

So, when the hero comes into the city, what do we expect?

Save Us, Please

As Matthew's story continues, the crowds both in front of Jesus and behind him shouted out: "Hosanna to the Son of David! Blessed is the one who comes in the name of the Lord! Hosanna in the highest heaven!" (Matthew 21:9).

"Hosanna" is a Hebrew term that means, literally, "save, please," or in more formal terms, "Save, we pray." It is based on the same root we have already encountered in reference to Zechariah 9:9; it is the root that underlies the names Joshua, Hosea, and Jesus (which we can hear in Jesus' Aramaic name, Yeshu or Yeshua).

More than just an exhortation, "hosanna" is a reference to Psalm 118, one of the Hallel Psalms (113–118) that pilgrims would sing as they came to Jerusalem, and as Jews would recite on the Passover holiday. To this day the Hallel Psalms are chanted in synagogues on the first two days of Passover, on Shavuot (the second pilgrimage festival in antiquity), on Sukkot (the Festival of

Booths, the third pilgrimage holiday in antiquity), on Hanukkah, and on several other holidays. The Psalms celebrate the Exodus, the miracle of the parting of the waters at the Red Sea, the giving of the Torah at Mount Sinai, the resurrection of the dead, and the Messianic Age.

The Hebrew word *Hallel* means "to praise," and you have probably guessed that it is part of the word *Hallelujah*, which is literally an imperative: "praise you (all), Yah(weh)." Psalm 118 both begins and ends with the line, "O give thanks to the Lord, for he is good; his steadfast love endures forever!" (vv. 1, 29). Verse 25 reads: "Save us, we beseech you, O Lord! O Lord, we beseech you," and verse 26 continues, "Blessed is the one who comes in the name of the Lord."

Other verses in this first psalm have also found a role in Christian Scripture and liturgy. Psalm 118:22-23 is quoted several times in the New Testament: "The stone that the builders rejected has become the chief cornerstone. This is the Lord's doing, it is marvelous in our eyes." The next verse, 118:24, is the well-known line, "This is the day that the Lord has made; let us rejoice and be glad in it."

The references to hosannas should remind the listeners of grace and beauty and promise of the Hallel Psalms, and you may want to look up on your own the rest of Psalm 118 as well as Psalms 113–118. Matthew clearly knew how to write a gospel!

But the Psalms not only ask for salvation; they also show that salvation is in a sense already present. We don't have to pin all our hopes on a hero and invest all our yearnings toward some future date. *This* is the day for rejoicing; any time the psalm is sung, this is the day. The kingdom of heaven is present here, if we just pay attention.

And so we might wonder: from what do we seek salvation?

From sin, yes. But also from pain, from despair, from loneliness, from poverty, from oppression. We are all in need of some form of salvation. Indeed, the idea of salvation for most of the Scriptures of Israel is not about spiritual matters, but physical ones:

God hears our cries.
And the stories remind us that people, still, cry out to be saved.

the Passover, the setting of the Passion narrative, is about salvation from slavery. God hears our cries. And the stories remind us that people, still, cry out to be saved. Will our cries be heard by others? Will we hear the cries of others? Will God act? Will we?

Son of David

Finally, Matthew depicts the crowds as praising Jesus and calling him "Son of David" (21:9). The reference is more to the great king who brings the ark to Jerusalem (think Gregory Peck or Richard Gere in the remake). The recollection of David is a reminder of God's promises concerning a rule of peace and safety, justice and compassion.

The Gospels are celebrating Jesus coming into his own city. He has already been identified as the son of David; we've known this since Matthew's genealogy and then the Christmas story. We've seen Jesus hailed as Son of David by two men who are blind (Matthew 9:27), by the crowds who marvel at the healing of a man who was both blind and mute (Matthew 12:23), by the Canaanite woman whose daughter Jesus relieves of an evil spirit (Matthew 15:22), and by two blind men, on the side of the road, who hear of his coming (Matthew 20:30). When we hear "Son of David," the message is one of sight to the blind, voice to the mute, and peace to the possessed. We might also think of the actual "son of David" named in Matthew's genealogy, Solomon, the king known for his wisdom, and for seeking the wisdom of others, such as the Queen of Sheba.

More, Jerusalem is David's capital, so Jesus the son of David is coming to claim what is for the Gospels rightfully his.

The crowd—again, that's us—knows what it wants. It wants what we all want. It wants political reform; it wants a meek king; it wants compassion rather than conquest. It wants a balanced budget, affordable health care, a strong military, clean water, peaceful streets, lower taxes, good schools. . . . But leaders cannot do everything on their own. We've already seen how the Psalms insist that kings must rely on God. They must also rely on the people to carry out God's will. As we praise a king, a Son of David, we should also ask how much are *we* willing to contribute in order to achieve these goals; how much are we willing to take responsibility, to work, to sacrifice?

I am reminded of a scene from the musical *Hello, Dolly!* where Dolly sings the song, "Before the Parade Passes By." Early on she sings, "I've gotta get in step while there's still time left." Dolly, who finds that her own life is passing by without fulfillment, realizes she can't just stand on the sidelines. She sings of longing for something to reach for and to motivate her: "I wanna feel my heart coming alive again." This should be our response to Jesus' entry into Jerusalem. Something long known but not yet experienced, something exciting, revelatory, is coming. And we are called into the procession of justice, of compassion, of peace, of a vision of the kingdom of heaven, the kingdom as God wants it to be.

Jerusalem

Matthew 21:10-11, the last verses of our story, read, "When he entered Jerusalem, the whole city was in turmoil, asking, 'Who is this?' The crowds were saying, 'This is the prophet Jesus from Nazareth in Galilee.'" The response is both accurate and incomplete, and it is another testimony to Matthew's art. The reference to the prophet is an allusion to Deuteronomy 18:18, where God says, "I will raise up for them a prophet like [Moses] from among their own people; I will put my words in the mouth of the prophet, who shall speak to them everything that I command." Thus, Matthew has associated Jesus with the meek king predicted in Zechariah, through that allusion with the meek Moses, with King David, and now with a prophet like Moses.

When our expectations are high, when the hype has reached exponential proportions, of course we are shaken up. All the planning, all the sacrifices, all the waiting are finally paying off. The time has come to bring about the kingdom of heaven. The Triumphal Entry has arrived, and so we rejoice.

But a shaky crowd is not a stable one. Our hopes may be dashed, and it may turn out that those years of planning are not the end, but only the beginning. As Jesus is entering Jerusalem, with the crowds, from Nazareth in Galilee, so too Pilate is entering Jerusalem with his soldiers. The confrontation is inevitable.

According to Matthew, Jesus is a combination of David and Moses, the meek king and the good planner, the crowd favorite and the Son of God. And yet, David faced a civil war when his own son, Absalom, rebelled. Moses faced rejection from his own people; indeed, that very passage in Numbers 12 which describes him as "meek" begins with his siblings, Aaron and Miriam, questioning his leadership. Yes, Moses and David are heroes, and so no wonder Jesus, associated with both, gets the acclamation and the hosannas. But we should also remember that today's hero may be tomorrow's victim. Crowds are fickle. Even children or siblings can become the enemy. In Matthew 10:21, Jesus warns, "Brother will betray brother to death, and a father his child, and children will rise against parents and have them put to death." Jesus will be denied by Peter and betrayed by Judas; he knows what it is like to have "family" turn against him.

The whole Triumphal Entry scene is one of anticipation, but it cannot be read alone. The parade into Jerusalem, with all the hype and hope, leads directly to the cross.

Earlier in Matthew's Gospel, Jesus not only predicts his suffering, death, and vindication, he tells his followers: "If any want to become my followers, let them deny themselves and take up their cross and follow me" (16:24). Today we have the common expression, "We all have our crosses to bear," a term used from the most ordinary things, like, "I have to take out the garbage or do the dishes," to the very serious, such as, "I've just lost my job" or "I've been diagnosed with cancer." The former examples are silly and trivial; the latter, serious and tragic.

But neither quite gets at the meaning of taking up one's cross at the time of Jesus: To take up the cross meant to risk Roman capital punishment. It meant being willing to accept hardships and loss, humiliation and imprisonment, even death, in order to proclaim a vision of a better world, a divine kingdom, and then to work for it. The Triumphal Entry cannot be separated from the cross, and the cross cannot be separated from the call of justice. And that call cannot be separated from risk, personal, professional, permanent.

A triumphal entry is a military parade. It's a sign of a conquering commander coming into the city and celebrating his victory. But all victories, to this point, come at a cost: of devastation to the land, to the buildings, to the people. William Tecumseh Sherman, who commanded the Union troops at the first Battle of Bull Run in 1861 and the Battle at Shiloh in 1862 and who captured Atlanta in 1864, proclaimed, "War is hell." When the victorious general rides through the town and we attend the parade, we should remember the blood, and the deaths, that come in his wake.

And yet we recall that David faced rebellion in his own household; Moses faced rejection by his own people. They are not alone. Cain killed Abel, Jacob feared that his brother, Esau, would kill him; Joseph was sold into slavery by his brothers....Jesus reminds us of these ancient figures, in both their triumphs and their tragedies. And we remember that Jesus, the meek king, offers a different path to victory than that of the typical conquering hero. The blood that will be spilled, the life that will be taken, will be his own.

Politically and historically, for Jesus to come into the city and have people hail him as son of David or conquering king is dangerous. Rome's agents, including the governor, Pontius Pilate, recognize that when the crowds hail a new hero, they are also challenging Roman authority. First-century Jewish historian Josephus, a contemporary of Jesus, tells us that Herod Antipas killed John the Baptizer because he was afraid of this popular teacher. Writing in the second half of the first century CE, Josephus tells us, "Now, when [many] others came in crowds about him, for they were greatly moved [or pleased] by hearing his words, Herod, who feared lest the great influence John had over the people might put it into his power and inclination to raise a rebellion (for they seemed ready to do anything he should advise), thought it best, by putting him to death, to prevent any mischief he might cause, and not bring himself into difficulties, by sparing a man who might make him repent of it when it should be too late."* John's death was thus a preemptive strike. And Jesus was well aware that Herod had beheaded John.

Incidentally, none of the Gospel accounts of Jesus' entry into the city flags the Romans as the major danger, even though Jesus dies on a Roman cross, with the Roman charge, "King of the Jews," affixed to the titulus.

Matthew's story of the Triumphal Entry ends with the crowds affirming, "This is the prophet Jesus from Nazareth in Galilee" (Matthew 21:11) and then Jesus entering into the Temple where his violent actions bring him to the attention of the "chief priest and scribes."

Mark's version of the Triumphal Entry signals the risk in a way Matthew doesn't. Mark tells us, following the hosannas, that Jesus "entered Jerusalem and went into the temple; and when he had looked around at everything, as it was already late, he went out to Bethany with the twelve" (Mark 11:11). The next day, he will see the fig tree, fail to find figs on it, and curse it. *Then* Jesus enters the Temple. Jesus is not only about to claim Jerusalem as his own, he is about to claim the Temple, what he has called "my Father's house" in Luke 2:49 and in John 2:16. The next morning, *after* Jesus' action in the Temple, the disciples see that the cursed tree has withered to the root. "Then Peter remembered and said to him, 'Rabbi, look! The fig tree that you cursed has withered'" (Mark 11:21). The tree symbolizes the devastation of Jerusalem when, forty years later, the Romans besiege and then destroy the city. In Matthew's account, the day after Jesus enters Jerusalem and disrupts the Temple activities, Jesus sees the tree, curses it,

---

* Josephus, *Antiquities* 18.5.2.

and immediately the tree withers (see Matthew 21:18-20); same story, different version, like variations on a theme.

Luke ends the scene of the Triumphal Entry with some of the Pharisees saying to Jesus, "Teacher, order your disciples to stop." Jesus responds, "I tell you, if these were silent, the stones would shout out" (Luke 19:39-40). The move toward Jerusalem is inexorable; it cannot be stopped. Here we might wonder if we've attempted to silence anyone who is trying to be heard. Have we stopped up our ears from hearing the cries of those who ask for help, or have we turned a blind eye to those who need our attention?

Finally, John—who usually tells a quite different story than the ones we find in Matthew, Mark, and Luke, the so-called "Synoptic Gospels" (because they "see" [as in "optics"] "together" [as in "syn-thesis," or "syn-dicate," or "syn-chronicity"])—does not contain the story of Jesus' sending the disciples to find the donkey; for John, Jesus himself finds "a young donkey" and sits on it in fulfillment of Zechariah's prediction. Of greater import, only John mentions "branches of palm trees" (John 12:13). Readers familiar with the Jewish tradition would immediately be reminded of the pilgrimage feast *not* of Passover but of Sukkot, also known as "Booths" or "Tabernacles." Although the pilgrimage holidays of Passover, Shavuot, and Sukkot can no longer be celebrated by pilgrimage, since the Romans destroyed the Temple in 70 CE, Jews continue to celebrate these holidays in their homes and synagogues. On Sukkot, Jews—in synagogues to this day!—hold in their hands a *lulav*, the frond of a date palm, together with the branches of willow and myrtle trees. The palm reminds us of Psalm 92:12, "The righteous flourish like the palm tree" even as it fulfills the commandment of Leviticus 23:40, "On the first day [of the festival] you shall take the fruit of majestic trees, branches of palm trees, boughs of leafy trees, and willows of the brook; and you shall rejoice before the LORD your God for seven days."

The Feast of Sukkot not only commemorates the wanderings of the children of Israel in the wilderness, it also is—wait for it!—the setting of Zechariah 9–14, that very section where the prophet predicts, in 9:9, the king entering the city on a donkey. It is the time when, as Zechariah 12:10 puts it, God "will pour out a spirit of compassion and supplication on the house of David and the inhabitants of Jerusalem, so that when they look on the one whom they have pierced, they shall mourn for him, as one mourns for an only child, and weep bitterly over him, as one weeps over a firstborn." At the end of all this, Zechariah 14:16 proclaims, "Then all who survive of the nations that have come against Jerusalem shall go up year after year to worship the King, the LORD of hosts, and to keep the festival of booths." The palm branches send us from Passover to Sukkot, from redemption from slavery to the universal acclamation of God.

John concludes this fourth version of the story with two new points. First, John tells us that Jesus' disciples did not understand what they were seeing. Only after Jesus is resurrected do they recall "that these things had been written of him and had been done to him" (John 12:16). Only in light of the Resurrection can the rest of the story have its full meaning. In effect, John is telling us to go to the end of the Gospel, and then read it anew, over and over again. Each time we read, we will recollect moments that echo, from chapter to chapter. More, John encourages us to go back to the Scriptures of Israel, the Old Testament, and reread those books in light of the story of Jesus. And when we do, we find new things in old texts.

Second, John tells us that as the crowd, which had been following Jesus since the raising of Lazarus (see John 11, the previous chapter), continued to bear witness to Jesus' signs, the Pharisees, as they do in Luke, show concern: they say to one another, "Look, the world has gone after him!" (John 12:19). The triumph is inevitable, as is the cross.

The End of the Parade

Jesus is about to enter Jerusalem, and its Temple. Where are we? Are we in the parade and shouting "Hosanna!" or are we on the sidelines, afraid to take part?

When the election is over and the victory is won, now what? Do we expect miracles, or is now the time the work really begins? Can we do more than sing the songs? Can we walk the walk? Must we move so quickly from Palm Sunday to Easter Sunday, or can we take the time for Lent to do its work?

Where are we?
Are we in the parade and shouting "Hosanna!" or are we on the sidelines, afraid to take part?

What do we know now, and what might we learn if we looked again, at our Scripture, our lives, our world? Do we see it differently in the light of the good news?

Chapter 2

The Temple:
Risking Righteous Anger

Chapter 2

THE TEMPLE: RISKING RIGHTEOUS ANGER

Then they came to Jerusalem. And he entered the temple and began to drive out those who were selling and those who were buying in the temple, and he overturned the tables of the money changers and the seats of those who sold doves; and he would not allow anyone to carry anything through the temple. He was teaching and saying, "Is it not written,

> *'My house shall be called a house of prayer for all the nations'?*
> *But you have made it a den of robbers."*

And when the chief priests and the scribes heard it, they kept looking for a way to kill him; for they were afraid of him, because the whole crowd was

*spellbound by his teaching. And when evening
came, Jesus and his disciples went out of the city.*

Mark 11:15-19

*The Passover of the Jews was near, and Jesus went
up to Jerusalem. In the temple he found people
selling cattle, sheep, and doves, and the money
changers seated at their tables. Making a whip
of cords, he drove all of them out of the temple,
both the sheep and the cattle. He also poured out
the coins of the money changers and overturned
their tables. He told those who were selling the
doves, "Take these things out of here! Stop making
my Father's house a marketplace!" His disciples
remembered that it was written, "Zeal for your
house will consume me." The Jews then said to
him, "What sign can you show us for doing this?"
Jesus answered them, "Destroy this temple, and
in three days I will raise it up." The Jews then
said, "This temple has been under construction
for forty-six years, and will you raise it up in
three days?" But he was speaking of the temple of
his body.*

John 2:13-21

There is clearly risk involved in what Jesus does in the
Temple. People notice. The Temple has police. He could have
been arrested.

There is risk for us as well, for we find that the scene known
as the "Cleansing of the Temple" in the Synoptic Gospels
(Matthew, Mark, and Luke) is substantially different than what

the Gospel of John tells us. For the Synoptics, the Temple cleansing comes on the heels of the Triumphal Entry. If that first victory parade did not threaten the powers-that-be, the Roman governor and the high priest responsible for keeping the peace of Jerusalem, the Temple incident would. Yet for John, the Temple incident occurs in chapter 2, at the beginning of Jesus' ministry, right after he turned water into wine at Cana. There is no political threat here. More, what Jesus says and does in the Temple differs.

In this chapter, we'll look closely at what Mark and John tell us, and we'll introduce the distinct points present in Matthew and Luke. A number of my students get very worried when I point out the differences. They fear that they cannot trust the Gospels, or that Matthew or John somehow got the details wrong. There are some biblical studies experts who delight in pointing out discrepancies in the texts, as if a different perspective would serve like a thread that, when pulled, would unravel the entire picture. Nonsense! The Gospel writers are telling their readers what they think the readers need to know. And the people who put the biblical canon together determined that four separate stories are better than one. The differing details give us different insights, because they present the same story from different perspectives. We should rejoice in the distinctions, and in the wisdom of the people who put the New Testament together and who allowed different perspectives on the story to be retained.

This same approach to celebrating rather than attempting to harmonize everything was already established by the canonizers of the Scriptures of Israel. There are two creation narratives (Genesis 1:1–2:4a; Genesis 2:4b–3:24), there are two versions of the death of the Philistine champion Goliath, there are two versions of the census that David took, and so on. And as we have just seen, the four Gospels have different emphases in the story of the Triumphal Entry. How do we appreciate each text on its own? How can we, in our increasingly hurried society, take the time to read slowly, and listen closely?

The incident known as the "Cleansing of the Temple" is described in all four Gospels. Most people have the idea—probably from Hollywood—that this is a huge disruption. When we see this scene depicted in movies, we find Jesus fuming with anger, and we inevitably see gold coins falling down in slow motion. Everything in the Temple comes to a standstill. Not all the movies actually have Jesus speaking at this moment, perhaps because they think that actions are, at least here, more important than words; perhaps because if they include both what he says in the Synoptics and what he says in John, the incident becomes confusing or even too long. But we are not watching a movie; we are studying the Gospels.

The Jerusalem Temple, which King Herod the Great began to rebuild and which was still under construction at the time of Jesus, had several courts.

Here's what we know about the actual setting. We begin by noting that the Temple complex was enormous. It was the size of twelve soccer fields put end to end. So, if Jesus turns over a table or two in one part of the complex, it's not going to make much of a difference given the size of the place. The action therefore did not stop all business; it is symbolic rather than practical. Our responsibility is to determine what was symbolized. For that, we need to know how the Temple functioned.

The Jerusalem Temple, which King Herod the Great began to rebuild and which was still under construction at the time of Jesus, had several courts. The inner sanctum, known as the "Holy of Holies," is where the high priest entered, only on Yom Kippur, the Day of Atonement, to ask for forgiveness for himself and for the people. Outside of that was the Court of the Priests, then the Court of Israel, the Court of the Women, and then the Court of the Gentiles, who were welcome to worship in the Temple.

The outer court, the Court of the Gentiles, is where the vendors sold their goods. The Temple at the time of Jesus was many things: it was a house of prayer for all nations; it was the site for the three pilgrimage festivals of Passover, Shavuot/Pentecost, and Sukkot/Booths; it was a symbol of Jewish tradition (we might think of it as comparable, for the Jewish people of the time, to how Americans might view the Statue of Liberty); it was the national bank; and it was the only place in the Jewish world where sacrifices could be offered. Therefore, there needed to be vendors on site. Pilgrims who sought to offer doves (such as Mary and Joseph do, following the birth of Jesus, according to Luke 2:24) or a sheep for the Passover meal would not bring the animals with them from Galilee or Egypt or Damascus. They would not risk the animal becoming injured and so unfit for sacrifice. The animal might fly or wander away, be stolen, or die. And, as one of my students several years ago remarked, "The pilgrims might get hungry on the way." One bought one's offering from the vendors. And, despite Hollywood, and sermon after sermon, there is no indication that the vendors were overcharging or exploiting the population. The people would not have allowed that to happen. Thus, Jesus is *not* engaging in protest of cheating the poor.

Next, we need to think of the Temple as something other than what we think of churches. A church, usually, is a place of quiet and decorum. In many congregations, children come to the front for a story and then are dismissed from the main area so that they can have religious education (or cookies, or both), and the adults can listen more closely to the sermon. The Temple was something much different: It was a tourist attraction, especially during the pilgrimage festivals. It was very crowded, and it was noisy. The noise was loud and boisterous, and because it was Passover, people were happy because they were celebrating the Feast of Freedom. For many, it was one of the few opportunities to celebrate by eating meat rather than just fish. We might think of the setting as a type of vacation for the pilgrims: a chance to leave their homes, to catch up with friends and relatives, to see the "big city," and to feel a special connection with their fellow Jews and with God. It is into this setting that Jesus comes.

Driving Out the Vendors

Matthew tells us that "Jesus entered the temple and drove out all who were selling and buying in the temple, and he overturned the tables of the money changers and the seats of those who sold doves" (21:12). Mark, who alone notes that Jesus had scouted out the Temple the day of the Triumphal Entry, adds that "he would not allow anyone to carry anything through the temple" (11:16). Luke drops out the reference to the money changers and efficiently notes, "Then he entered the temple and began to drive out those who were selling things there" (Luke 19:45). Finally, John tells us, "In the temple he found people selling cattle, sheep, and doves, and the money changers seated at their tables. Making a whip of cords, he drove all of them out of the temple, both the sheep and the cattle. He also poured out the coins of the money changers and overturned their tables" (2:14-15).

In all cases but especially in John's Gospel, Jesus appears violent. We might think of his action in terms of righteous anger or even *holy anger*. There are times, we may find, that business as usual is not only inappropriate, it is obscene. Something has to be done. If we do not become angry when we see images of suffering children, if we do not feel some sort of rage when preventable tragedies occur, if we do not feel compelled to act, then something has gone terribly wrong, with us.

Some of my students insist that anger is a sin. I think whether it is a sin depends on the type of anger we manifest. It is true that the "wrath" is among the classical "seven deadly sins" (the others are pride, greed, lust, envy, gluttony, and sloth). But "wrath" here refers to a temper out of control, to rage, and so to hate and the desire for revenge. That is not the same thing as righteous anger. Righteous anger seeks restitution, not revenge; it seeks correction, not retribution.

We can see the different types of anger manifested in the Gospels: Jesus forbids anger against a person. In the Sermon on the Mount (Matthew 5:22), he states, "I say to you that if you are angry with a brother or sister, you will be liable to judgment; and if you insult a brother or sister, you will be liable to the council; and if you say, 'You fool,' you will be liable to the hell of fire." The anger he forbids is anger against another person. But he does not forbid anger against systemic evils: hypocrisy, exploitation, harassment, molestation, drug pushing, and so on. Such forms of injustice should make us angry, and that anger should lead to constructive action.

It seems to me that Jesus, in the Temple, was angry. But what so angered him? I hear from a number of people, whether my students in class or congregations who have invited me to speak with them, that the Temple must have been a dreadful institution; that it exploited the poor; that it was in cahoots with Rome; that Caiaphas, the High Priest in charge of the Temple, was a terrible person; that it banned Gentiles from worship and so displayed hatred of foreigners; and so forth. A few suggest that there was a "Temple Domination System" that represented everything wrong with society. Some tell me that the Temple imposed oppressive purity laws that forbade people from entering, and so Jesus, who rejected those laws, rejected the Temple as well. No wonder Jesus wanted to destroy the institution.

But none of these views fits what we know about either Jesus or history.

First, Jesus did not hate the Temple, and he did not reject it. If he did, then it makes no sense that his followers continued to worship there. Jesus himself calls the Temple "my Father's house" (Luke 2:49; John 2:16). We see in the book of Acts, for example, that Paul goes into the Temple frequently and participates in Temple ritual. And Paul makes explicit in his Epistle to the Romans that Temple worship is God-given and good (Romans 9:4; "worship" refers to the Temple service).

Second, Jesus is not opposed to purity laws. To the contrary, he *restores* people to states of ritual purity. Even more, he tells a man whom he has cured of leprosy, "Go, show yourself to the priest, and offer for your cleansing what Moses commanded, as a testimony to them" (Mark 1:44; see also Matthew 8:4; Luke 5:14).

Third, Jesus says nothing about the Temple exploiting the population. As we'll see in the next chapter, when we talk about the widow who makes an offering of her two coins, Jesus is concerned not with what the Temple charges, but with the generosity of the worshipers.

Fourth, we've already seen that the Temple has an outer court, where Gentiles are welcome to worship. They were similarly welcome in the synagogues of antiquity, and today. They do not have the same rights and responsibilities as do Jews, and that makes sense as well. When I visit a church, there are certain things I may not do. We might also think of how nations function: Canadians, for example, cannot do certain things in the USA, such as vote for president; nor can citizens of the USA vote in Canadian elections.

As for Caiaphas, he deserves a chapter of his own (as do, for example, Judas, Pontius Pilate, Nicodemus, Joseph of Arimathea, the centurion at the cross, and pretty much everyone else who appears in the Passion narrative). We can, however, note the following: Caiaphas's job was to keep the peace. Because Judea is under direct Roman rule and there is no ruling king, Caiaphas represents the people of Judea to Rome. He is appointed, as were other high priests since Rome took over Judea completely in 6 CE, by the Romans and serves at their pleasure. More, the Roman governor keeps control of the high priestly vestments, so Caiaphas can only do his job if Pilate lets him.

Caiaphas is basically between a rock and a hard place. He is the nominal head of Judea, and he is supposed to keep the peace. Judea is occupied by Rome, and Roman soldiers are stationed there. Caiaphas needs to make sure that these soldiers do not go on the attack. He needs to placate Pilate, and he needs to placate Rome.

At the same time, as the High Priest, he has a responsibility to the Jewish tradition. Rome wanted the Jews to offer sacrifices to the emperor. The emperor was considered to be a god, but Caiaphas and the other Jews refused to participate in this type of offering because they would not worship the emperor. The most they were willing to do was offer sacrifice *on behalf of* the emperor and the empire.

Caiaphas also has to put up with Pilate, the prefect of Judea and representative of Rome. Pilate raided the Temple treasury in order to build the aqueduct, but that was money that was supposed to have been used for Temple expenses, including to help support people who used the Temple or needed food.

When Jesus comes into the city in the Triumphal Entry, when people are hailing him as son of David, Caiaphas recognizes the political danger. The Gospel of John tells us that the people wanted to make Jesus king (John 6:15). Caiaphas has to watch out for the mob. Caiaphas also has to watch out for all these Jewish pilgrims coming from all over the empire celebrating the Feast of Freedom, the end of slavery. When he sees Roman troops surrounding the Temple Mount, Caiaphas has to keep the peace. And Jesus is a threat to that peace. But none of this has to do directly with Jesus' actions in the Temple. He is not at this point protesting Caiaphas's role.

Sometimes I hear people say that Jesus drove the "money lenders" out of the Temple. That's wrong, too. Money-lending was a business into which the medieval church forced Jews, because the church concluded that charging interest was unnatural (money should not beget money). Yet people needed, then and now, to take out loans. The issue for the Gospel is not money *lending* but money *changing*: these money changers exchanged the various currencies of the Roman Empire into Tyrian shekels, the type of silver coin that the Temple accepted. We experience the same process when we visit a foreign country and have to exchange our money for the local currency.

So, if Jesus is not condemning the Temple itself, or financial exploitation, or purity practices, what is he condemning? Let's look at what the Gospels actually say.

House of Prayer for All Nations

According to Matthew, Mark, and Luke (remember, the Synoptic Gospels "see alike" and so tell the same basic story), the concern is not the Temple, but the attitude of the people who are coming to it. In Mark's account Jesus begins by saying, "Is it not written, 'My house shall be called a house of prayer for all the nations'?" (11:17). Indeed, it is so written. Jesus is here condensing and then quoting Isaiah 56:6-7: "And the foreigners who join themselves to the LORD, to minister to him, to love the name of the LORD, and to be his servants, all who keep the sabbath and do not profane it, and hold fast my covenant—these I will bring to my holy mountain, and make them joyful in my house of prayer; their burnt offerings and their sacrifices will be accepted on my altar; for my house shall be called a house of prayer for all peoples." Jesus' rhetorical question should be answered with a resounding "Yes!"—for the Temple already was a house of prayer for all people. More, he is standing in the Court of the Gentiles when he makes his pronouncement.

Gentiles were welcome in the Temple. In fact, the Temple was open to everyone. Men, women, slaves, Jews, Gentiles, free people, rich people, poor people—the Temple was a house of prayer for everyone, and everyone was supposed to feel welcome.

There were, however, boundaries that Gentiles were not to cross. Torah mandates that one must "love your neighbor as yourself" and "love the stranger who dwells among you, because you were strangers in the land of Egypt" (Leviticus 19:18, 34; author's translation): thus, there are fellow Jews and there are strangers, but love encompasses all. We might think, as a possible comparison, of churches that restrict certain rites to baptized members of those churches. When I am in a church service, which is often, I cannot participate in Communion, but I am still (usually) warmly welcomed. Should I convert, however, I would have the same rights, and rites, as church members. Thus, the problem is not that the Temple excludes Gentiles.

Already we find the challenge, and the risk. Are churches today houses of prayer for all people, or are they just for people who look like us, walk like us, and talk like us? How do we make other people feel welcome? Is the stranger greeted upon walking into the church? Is the first thing a stranger hears in the sanctuary, "You're in my seat"? When we pray or sing hymns, do we think of what those words would sound like in a stranger's ears?

I've been invited to many churches over the year. Sometimes, after doing an adult education program, and sometimes a youth program, I'll stay for the service. Once I find my way to the sanctuary, I sit in the back so I don't disrupt anyone or get in the way of a procession or Communion. There are numerous times I have entered the church and not a single person has said, "Hello, are you new? Would you like to sit next to me?" When people "pass the peace" or simply, when instructed, greet other members of the congregation, I've turned to shake the hand of the person next to me in the pew, or behind me, and been ignored. Or, perhaps just as bad, the hand is extended but there is no eye contact, no actual recognition that they are actually welcoming a stranger. How do we make the church feel like a house of prayer for all nations, which means everyone's supposed to be welcome?

Matthew and Luke drop out "for all nations," and appropriately so, for they knew it already was a house of prayer for all nations. Matthew and Luke thus change the focus to one of prayer. And prayer gets us closer to what is going on in the Synoptic tradition.

Den of Thieves

Jesus continues, "But you are making it a den of robbers" (Matthew 21:13). Here he is quoting Jeremiah 7:11: "Has this house, which is called by my name, become a den of robbers in your sight?" A "den of robbers" (sometimes translated a "den of thieves") is not where robbers rob. "Den" really means "cave," and a cave of robbers is where robbers go after they have taken what does not belong to them, and count up their loot. The context of Jeremiah's quotation—and remember, it always helps to look up the context of citations to the Old Testament—tells us this. Jeremiah 7:9-10 depicts the ancient prophet as condemning the people of his own time, the time right before Babylonians destroyed Solomon's Temple over five hundred years earlier: "Will you steal, murder, commit adultery, swear falsely, make offerings to Baal, and go after other gods that you have not known, and then come and stand before me in this house, which is called by my name, and say, 'We are safe!'—only to go on doing all these abominations?"

Some people in Jeremiah's time, and at the time of Jesus, and today, take divine mercy for granted and see worship as an opportunity to show off new clothes rather than recommit to clothing the naked. The present-day comparison to what Jeremiah, and Jesus, condemned is easy to make: The church member sins during the workweek, either by doing what is wrong or by failing to do what is right. Then on Sunday morning this same individual, perhaps convinced of personal righteousness, heartily sings the hymns, happily shakes the hands of others, and generously puts a fifty-dollar bill in the collection plate. That makes the church a den of robbers—a cave of sinners. It becomes a safe place for those who are not truly repentant and who do not truly follow what Jesus asks. The church becomes a place of showboating, not of fishing for people.

Jeremiah and Jesus indicted people then, and now. The ancient Temple, and the present-day church, should be places where people not only find community, welcome the stranger, and repent of their sins. They should be places where people promise to live a godly life, and then keep their promises.

The ancient Temple, and the present-day church, should be places where people not only find community, welcome the stranger, and repent of their sins. They should be places where people promise to live a godly life, and then keep their promises.

Maybe, perhaps during Lent, congregants might stop the church's "business as usual," and *really* make others feel welcome. Maybe congregants might fully assess what they have done during the past year and what they will do in the future. Have they forgiven trespasses, or resisted temptation? Have they loved their neighbors as themselves? In some churches, congregants "pass the sign of peace": Have they, as Jesus also mandates, loved their enemies? Have they shaken the hand of the person they do not like or who does not like them? Have they fully been reconciled not only to God but also to one another?

Stop Making My Father's House a Marketplace

John's Gospel says nothing about the house of prayer or den of robbers. In John's Gospel, Jesus starts not simply by overturning the tables, but also by using a "whip of cords" (since weapons were not permitted in the Temple, he may have fashioned the whip from straw at hand), and driving out the vendors. Jesus then says to the dove sellers, "Take these things out of here! Stop making my Father's house a marketplace!" (John 2:16). He is alluding to Zechariah 14:21, the last verse from this prophet, "and every cooking pot in Jerusalem and Judah shall be sacred to the LORD of hosts, so that all who sacrifice may come and use them to boil the flesh of the sacrifice. And there shall no longer be traders in the house of the LORD of hosts on that day."

In John's version of the Temple incident, Jesus anticipates the time when there will no longer be a need for vendors, for every house not only in Jerusalem but in all of Judea shall be like the Temple itself. The sacred nature of the Temple will spread through all the people. He sounds somewhat like the Pharisees here, since the Pharisees were interested in extending the holiness of the Temple to every household. The message is a profound one: Can our homes be as sanctified, as filled with worship, as the local church? Do we "do our best" on Sunday from 11 a.m. to 12 noon, but just engage in business as usual during the workweek? Do we pray only in church, or is prayer part of our daily practice? Do we celebrate the gifts of God only when it is time to do so in the worship service, or do we celebrate these gifts morning to night? Is the church just a building, or is the church the community who gathers in Jesus' name, who acts as Jesus taught, who lives the good news?

Jesus' words, citing Zechariah, do *even more*. They anticipate a time when all peoples, all nations, can worship in peace, and in love. There is no separation between home and house of worship, because the entire land lives in a sanctified state. Perhaps we can even hear a hint of Jeremiah's teaching of the "new covenant," when "no longer shall they teach one another, or say to each other, 'Know the LORD,' for they shall all know me, from the least of them to the greatest, says the LORD; for I will forgive their iniquity, and remember their sin no more" (Jeremiah 31:34). Can we envision this? Can we work toward it?

John's story of the Temple does not stop here.

Zeal for Your House

In John's account, the disciples provide their own interpretation of what they have just witnessed. Again, they find that Jesus is acting in full accordance with the Scriptures of Israel, as they remember Psalm 69:9, "It is zeal for your house that has consumed me." The disciples know their Scripture, and they are able to see new things in this ancient text in light of their encounter with Jesus. We might take the time to look at the full psalm—which is fairly long. And if we do, we'll recognize another verse from it, alluded to at the cross. Psalm 69:21b reads, "For my thirst they gave me vinegar to drink." The psalm is a "Psalm of lament," like the famous Psalm 22, which begins, "My God, my God, why have you forsaken me?" (v. 1).

And so, we stop again and ask, "What consumes us?" For what do we display "zeal"? For the football team? Movie stars? Our schools? Cars? How clean our home is? Jesus talked about finding the "pearl of great price": what is ours?

But He Was Speaking of the Temple of His Body

John's Temple scene concludes when Jesus says, "Destroy this temple, and in three days I will raise it up" (2:19). The sentence is a difficult one. It would be like saying, "Destroy the Statue of Liberty, and I'll have it back in place in seventy-two hours." The people listening, appropriately, question the comment. They note,

"This temple has been under construction for forty-six years, and will you raise it up in three days?" (2:20). It's a good question.

It turns out that Jesus had changed the subject. As John tells us, "he was speaking of the temple of his body" (2:21). We find a similar comment in the Synoptic Gospels. In Mark 14:58 Jesus states, "I will destroy this temple that is made with hands, and in three days I will build another, not made with hands," and in Matthew 26:61, he is said to have claimed, "I am able to destroy the temple of God and to build it in three days." Witnesses remember these words at the cross: they taunt Jesus, "You who would destroy the temple and build it in three days" (Mark 15:29; Matthew 27:40). John tells us that Jesus was talking about his body; the Synoptics leave the identity of this temple open.

Here, history helps us, a lot. Passion Week happened sometime during the governorship of Pontius Pilate, who ruled Judea from 26–36 CE. Jesus dies sometime between those dates; 33 CE, the traditional date, is historically plausible. The Roman army led by Titus destroyed the Temple in 70 CE. John, writing after the destruction of the Temple, knew this.

Jesus may well have predicted the destruction of the Temple. Jeremiah had done so, half a millennium before, and his prediction came true when the Babylonians took Jerusalem. Nor was Jesus the only one to predict this destruction. But for the earliest followers of Jesus, Jews such as Peter and John, Mary and Martha, Paul and Timothy, the Temple was still their house of prayer. They worshiped Jesus as Lord, and they worshiped as well in what Jesus called "my Father's house." When the Temple was destroyed, they, like their fellow Jews, continued to worship in their homes and in their synagogues.

The Jewish followers of Jesus took comfort in the idea that Jesus' body was for them a new temple. In the sacrifice of Jesus, and in eating the bread and drinking the wine, they could find the reconciliation that they had previously found in the Jerusalem Temple.

Paul talks about the followers of Jesus as the "body of Christ" and insists "that there may be no dissension within the body, but the members may have the same care for one another" (1 Corinthians 12:25). Paul also talks about the human body as a "temple of the Holy Spirit" (1 Corinthians 6:19). So, before we leave the Temple incident, we take one more step into Lent by thinking about bodies, the body of Jesus, and our own bodies.

Here are three things we might want to think about.

First, John tells us that Jesus' body is the New Temple. He will give his body to his followers as a sign of the new covenant, as a means of reconciliation, as a ransom for many. How should one respond to such extraordinary generosity?

Second, to take seriously the idea that the community gathered in Jesus' name *is* his body requires that this body be a welcome place for all people. Is it? Or is it a cave where robbers feel safe and outsiders feel unwelcome or threatened?

Third, the body is also the temple of the Holy Spirit, a point hinted at already in Genesis, which tells us that the human body is in the image and likeness of the divine. The Incarnation teaches that the divine takes on human flesh, and so that human body is of value. When we look at the face of our neighbor, or at our own images in the mirror, we see the face of the divine. And so, do we care for our bodies? This is Lent, the time when Christians around the world participate in acts of self-denial. Perhaps this is a time when those who enter into Lent start to think more seriously about how and what and with whom they eat. And that topic brings us later to the two suppers that are part of the Lenten story.

Chapter 3

Teachings:
Risking Challenge

Chapter 3

TEACHINGS: RISKING CHALLENGE

We've just seen Jesus disrupt business as usual in the Temple. In cases where such public action occurs, then and now, the police arrive quickly, calm the crowds, and arrest the offender. But no such arrest happens in any of our accounts. Mark tells us that after Jesus called the institution a "den of robbers," the chief priests "kept looking for a way to kill him; for they were afraid of him, because the whole crowd was spellbound by his teaching" (Mark 11:18). In this chapter, we look at several of Jesus' Temple teachings—the question of taxation; the "Greatest Commandment"; and the lesson of the "widow's mite."

There are other teachings, such as the question about the Resurrection, or the parables that Jesus tells in the Temple, that you may wish to explore on your own. Each of these episodes deserves a chapter—better, a book! We offer these reflections in the hopes that they will not only enrich your understanding of the passages but also spark you to self-reflection as we enter more fully into the Lenten season.

We start with the matter of teaching itself. Any time we teach, there's a risk of misunderstanding. I know from personal experience: there's always the possibility that someone in the classroom will misunderstand what I've said and come up with something completely off the wall. Then this student goes out into the world, gets up in the pulpit, and announces, "Professor Levine taught me...." It's terrifying! Teaching always carries risk. This is why the Epistle of James says, "not many of you should become teachers" (3:1).

Jesus takes many risks by teaching in the Temple, exponentially more than what I take in the classroom. His courage is extraordinary. He not only risks being misunderstood, he also risks being arrested. More, he is not only teaching people who want to learn; in the audience are some who want to trip him up with catch-22-type questions, and others who try to goad him into saying something controversial. Those Pharisees and Herodians who seek to trap him remind me of cocky students who sit in the back row and ask obnoxious or off-topic questions, not because they want to know the answers, but because they want to show off, to look clever or daring in the eyes of their neighbors, or to show that they in fact know more than the teacher does. Such students sometimes show up in my classroom, raise their hands, and ask their questions. But, given that I do know what I am doing and that I do not want to waste my time or that of the rest of the class, I answer in such a way that they never ask such obnoxious questions again.

I take my cues from Jesus here. First, try to figure out what is behind a question. Some questions are asked for reasons of cruelty or self-import, and not all questions deserve an answer.

In responding, I do my best not to sound rude or dismissive or insulting. I do not want to humiliate anyone in the classroom. On the other hand, I do not want to waste either my time or the time of the students who really want to learn more about Jesus and the Gospels. Thus, the question asked in a nasty or snarky way receives a patient answer, but one that clearly indicates I am aware of the attitude behind it. Second, know the Scriptures well. Third, make sure that, for seekers who are really interested in what you have to say, you respond with not only kindness and respect but also with empathy. Jesus is a master teacher, and in listening to him teach, I find I become a better teacher myself.

Taxation

Then the Pharisees went and plotted to entrap him in what he said. So they sent their disciples to him, along with the Herodians, saying, "Teacher, we know that you are sincere, and teach the way of God in accordance with truth, and show deference to no one; for you do not regard people with partiality. Tell us, then, what you think. Is it lawful to pay taxes to the emperor, or not?" But Jesus, aware of their malice, said, "Why are you putting me to the test, you hypocrites? Show me the coin used for the tax." And they brought him a denarius. Then he said to them, "Whose head is this, and whose title?" They answered, "The emperor's." Then he said to them, "Give therefore to the emperor the things that are the emperor's, and to God the things that are God's." When they

*heard this, they were amazed; and they left him
and went away.*

> Matthew 22:15-22 (*see also* Mark 12:13-17;
> Luke 20:20-26)

Taxation—a topic of discussion then and now. No politician can escape the questions of taxation; no politician should. But it's a rare politician who can get elected without promising to lower taxes (it may be even rarer for a politician who makes such a promise to know how to make up the shortfall). We question where our tax money should go: to the schools or to the military? for international aid or for local infrastructure? for raising the salaries of members of the Senate or for raising the minimum wage?

The question of taxation in first-century Jerusalem was even more difficult, for some of those taxes went not to provide services to the people, but to provide more money to the Roman Empire. Thus, the question is not "Should we pay taxes?" The question is "Is it lawful to pay taxes *to the emperor?*" We shall look at the various Synoptic accounts of this event; the details have minor differences, but the import is the same across the tradition.

The story starts with a trap. Matthew makes clear that the Pharisees and the Herodians don't care about the question of taxation; they care about making Jesus look bad in the eyes of the people. The opponents begin well enough by calling Jesus "teacher" (the Greek term here is *didaskalos*, which underlies the English word *didactic*). Then they say, ironically, what is true: they call Jesus "sincere," they affirm that he does "teach the way of God in accordance with the truth," and they praise him for not regarding "people with partiality." Put another way, he does not defer to anyone or, as my students will sometimes say, he does not suck up.

Given their acknowledgment of these attributes, we might think that these Pharisees and Herodians were followers of Jesus. But they are not. They are hypocrites, and their flattery is false.

Already we are on the alert: Do we praise Jesus in the church but then fail to act according to his teaching? Do we treat all people equally, or do we defer to the rich and the powerful, the clergy at the pulpit rather than the workers in the kitchen?

They are hypocrites, and their flattery is false. Already we are on the alert: Do we praise Jesus in the church but then fail to act according to his teaching?

Here's their question: "Is it lawful to pay taxes to the emperor, or not?" The reference is probably to the "head tax" based on Roman census information (we see hints of this in Luke 2:1-5, the census that brings Mary and Joseph to Bethlehem; despite the historical problems with Luke's story—another topic for another series—the fact that Rome collected taxes is certainly historical). Jesus now has a problem. If he says, "Don't pay your taxes," then Rome is going to exact swift retaliation. Anyone who rejects taxes to Caesar is Caesar's enemy, and the cross immediately looms in sight.

But if Jesus says, "Of course, pay your taxes," he will alienate a number of groups. He will alienate those who, whether for political reasons or religious reasons or both, think that Rome is in Judea illegitimately. He would alienate the freedom fighters who yearn for national autonomy (we might think of George Washington and others who fought in the American Revolution, whose slogan was, of course, "taxation without representation is tyranny!"). And he would alienate others who rejected Roman gods, Roman standards, Roman coinage, and the rest of the trappings of the pagan empire. How can we be a "priestly kingdom and a holy nation" (Exodus 19:6) if Rome is in charge and if our money is going to be spent on Roman temples and Roman armies? It may be such an attitude that lies behind the comment in John's Apocalypse: "no one can buy or sell who does not have the mark, that is, the name of the beast or the number of its name" (Revelation 13:17). If you can't buy or sell without adopting Roman values, get off the grid, go out into the desert, wait for the end of days. "Is it lawful to pay taxes to Caesar?" is a loaded question.

Jesus knows that they're putting him to this test, because Mark is very clear that Jesus "[knows] their hypocrisy" (Mark 12:15). Matthew makes the point starker by simply having Jesus call them "hypocrites." They don't care what the answer is. They just want to catch him saying something that at least will make parts of the crowd dislike him and, even better, bring the Romans in to arrest him and kill him.

According to Matthew, Jesus was "aware of their malice," but Mark offers a slightly different reading; in Mark, Jesus asks, "Why are you putting me to the test?" (Mark 12:15). Here we should pay attention to the "test language." The word in Greek for "test" is the same word sometimes translated as "tempt" or "trial" as in the "Our Father" prayer: "lead us not into temptation," or "do not bring us to the time of trial" (Matthew 6:13) or "do not bring us to the test" (author's translation). Jesus knows what it is like to be put to the test, and to be tempted, first by Satan, and now by these particular Pharisees and Herodians. He doesn't like it. No one would.

Then he says, "Bring me a denarius." A denarius is a nice chunk of change; it's a big silver coin. We'll see it mentioned again when we come to the story of a woman who anoints Jesus with ointment worth more than three hundred denarii (Mark 14:5). The denarius was a Roman coin engraved on one side with the image of Caesar. Although we cannot be sure exactly which coin Jesus' questioners displayed, the Gospel's first readers may well have thought of the denarius that had the picture of the emperor Tiberius on one side, with the inscription, in Latin, that translates, "Caesar Augustus Tiberius, son of the Divine [or Deified] Augustus." One did not have to know Latin to get the point. Augustus had been declared divine by the Roman Senate, and Tiberius is in his image. The other side was engraved with the depiction of a seated woman, probably Tiberius's wife, Julia, and the inscription, in Latin, *Pontif[ex] Maxim[us]*, which means "High Priest." Thus we have a contrast: the Roman "son of (a) god" and the Roman priestly system are associated with coinage; Jesus is not.

Why does Jesus ask them to show him a coin? Perhaps because Jesus is not carrying any money. In fact, we never see Jesus handling money. Even when he is asked if he pays the Temple tax in Matthew 17:24-27, he does not handle money but has Peter pay the tax for him (Peter finds the money, by the way, in the mouth of a fish; most other folks find their tax money in less exotic locations). Nor do we see Jesus distributing money to the poor. Jesus gives in kind—healing, exorcising, teaching— rather than in coin.

Next, Jesus specifically asks for "the coin used for the tax" (in Matthew 22:19) or more plainly "a denarius" (in Mark and Luke). He doesn't say, "Show me a coin"; he says, "Show me a denarius." He does this because a denarius has a picture of Caesar on it.

If the Pharisees want a kingdom of priests, a holy nation, then why are they carrying coinage with the emperor's image and proclaiming the emperor's divinity?

When I was little, I used to collect coins. When my dad would go to the bank, he'd always come back with 100 pennies. Then we'd look at the pennies together, the dates, where they were minted. Sometimes we'd find a wheat penny, and sometimes we'd find a more modern penny. I had this little coin booklet that had a space for every year (up to 1965—that was a long time ago!), and we'd put the penny for each year in its appropriate pocket. My dad would tell me stories about what happened for each year we'd find. We'd also talk about what we saw on the penny: stories of Abraham Lincoln, the Lincoln Memorial, the words *One Cent, In God we trust, E. Pluribus Unum,* and *The United States of America* (and I was expected to know all of those states, plus their capitals). Daddy made this a game; it was also an opportunity to learn about minting and about America.

In retrospect, I can see how these pennies were designed to reinforce patriotism. Caesar's image on the denarius reminds me how money can be propaganda. How does Rome—how does any government—show what it values? They put the images on coinage. Today, people are debating whether we should replace Andrew Jackson with a woman, perhaps Harriet Tubman, on the twenty-dollar bill. The denarius is Roman propaganda: it says that Caesar is divine, that Caesar has power, that Caesar has, and is, money. Power, divinity, and empire—they are all minted from the same mold. Jesus seeks a different mint, a different mold.

So he tells his inquisitors, "Give therefore to the emperor the things that are the emperor's, and to God the things that are God's" (Matthew 22:21). He doesn't actually answer the question—

rather, he poses a question of his own. He asks his questioners to determine what they think belongs to God and what they think belongs to Caesar. Luke also tells us that some people interpreted Jesus as saying that one should withhold tax money: at his trial, they accuse him by claiming, "We found this man perverting our nation, forbidding us to pay taxes to the emperor" (Luke 23:2). This would be an example of what might be called an "alternative fact." Words can be twisted, and teaching, as well any political statement, comes with risk.

What should we do regarding "taxes to the emperor"? For Jews in first-century Judea, living under Roman colonial rule, the decision was not easy. Exodus 9:29 proclaims, "The earth is the LORD's," and Psalm 24:1 repeats the refrain: "The earth is the LORD's and all that is in it, the world, and those who live in it." Therefore, everything belongs to God. Yet paying everything to God is not going to create safe roads or provide protection from marauding gangs or bring food to starving people. Josephus tells us that in the year 6 of the Common Era, Judas the Galilean staged a revolt against the Roman census, taken to establish the tax base. The Book of Acts mentions him. In Acts 5:37, Gamaliel, the Pharisee and member of the Sanhedrin, reminds the people of him: "Judas the Galilean rose up at the time of the census and got people to follow him; he also perished, and all who followed him were scattered." Gamaliel's point is to differentiate Jesus' followers from this earlier group.

"*Should* Rome receive tax money?" was a viable question for this earlier Judas, another Galilean leader, and it remained a question for Jesus' followers. For John the author of the Book of Revelation, the answer was no. John exhorts his followers to avoid having anything to do with Rome, which he calls "Babylon the great, mother of whores and of earth's abominations"

(Revelation 17:5). Paul is actually less clear on the topic than we have thought for generations. In Romans 13, Paul exhorts, "Let every person be subject to the governing authorities; for there is no authority except from God" (v. 1) and then asserts, "you also pay taxes, for the authorities are God's servants. . . . Pay to all what is due them—taxes to whom taxes are due, revenue to whom revenue is due" (13:6-7). It would have been nice had Paul actually identified these "authorities," and it is possible that he is not talking about state taxes at all. Rather, he may be talking about taxes paid to the Jerusalem Temple and perhaps fees paid to the local synagogue. By the time we get to 1 Peter, however, the teaching that followers of Jesus should pay the tax is in place. The author instructs, "Conduct yourselves honorably among the Gentiles, so that, though they malign you as evildoers, they may see your honorable deeds and glorify God when he comes to judge. For the Lord's sake accept the authority of every human institution, whether of the emperor as supreme" (1 Peter 2:12-13). For the author of 1 Peter, paying taxes is a means of protecting the community. Christians are not to worry about perceptions of supporting pagan views, because God knows what is in their hearts.

The question of paying taxes is a valid one today, particularly for people living under occupation, or under an unjust regime. It was a valid one in ancient Israel as well—how much does one go along with the emperor, and when must one resist?

The question of paying taxes is a valid one today, particularly for people living under occupation or under an unjust regime. It was a valid one in ancient Israel as well—how much does one go along with the emperor, and when must one resist? According to the Book of Daniel, King Nebuchadnezzar of Babylon "made a golden statue whose height was sixty cubits and whose width was six cubits" (one wonders how the thing stood up) and ordered all the "peoples, nations and languages" that at certain times, they were to "fall down and worship the golden statue" (Daniel 3:1-5). The penalty for refusal: being thrown into a fiery furnace. The famous trio of Shadrach, Meshach, and Abednego refused. Not all government proclamations should be obeyed.

And so we ask about our own responsibilities. If the governing authority is the Nazi Party, is it "lawful" in terms of what God would want to pay our taxes? Do we support the dictator? support unjust policies? Do we pay attention to where our tax dollars are going, or do we insist on such a "separation of Church and State" that we do whatever the government tells us, with "church" only being about the correct belief that gets us into heaven? Jesus tells us that how we act on earth makes a difference. He poses the question to us: what belongs to God, and what belongs to Caesar?

Jesus' questioners are stumped by his answer. There's no comeback. But the questions remain. As we enter into Lent, might we think about what we do with our money, and what is done, by others, with our money? Do we think about what our politicians stand for, since the question of taxes to the emperor cannot be divorced from the question of politics? What do we make of the relationship between the Church and the State? For what is each responsible? If we are to be our brother's (and sister's) keeper, then how do we show that necessary care?

Greatest Commandment

*One of the scribes came near and heard them
disputing with one another, and seeing that
he answered them well, he asked him, "Which
commandment is the first of all?" Jesus answered,
"The first is, 'Hear, O Israel: the Lord our God,
the Lord is one; you shall love the Lord your God
with all your heart, and with all your soul, and
with all your mind, and with all your strength.'
The second is this, 'You shall love your neighbor
as yourself.' There is no other commandment
greater than these." Then the scribe said to him,
"You are right, Teacher; you have truly said that
'he is one, and besides him there is no other'; and
'to love him with all the heart, and with all the
understanding, and with all the strength,' and
'to love one's neighbor as oneself,'—this is much
more important than all whole burnt offerings
and sacrifices." When Jesus saw that he answered
wisely, he said to him, "You are not far from the
kingdom of God." After that no one dared to ask
him any question.*

Mark 12:28-34 (see also Matthew 22:34-40)

Jewish tradition recognizes 613 commandments in the
Scriptures of Israel. One rabbinic tradition, found in the Talmud
(*Makkot* 24a) explains that there are 365 negative commandments
or prohibitions (for example, "You shall not kill" and "You shall
not commit adultery") that correspond to the number of days of
the [solar] year, and 248 positive commandments (for example,

"Honor your father and mother" and "Remember the Sabbath and keep it holy") corresponding to the number of a person's limbs.[*]

In addition to the list of ten commandments with which most of us are familiar (Exodus 20:1-17), these other commandments range from the equally familiar, "Love your neighbor as yourself" and "love the stranger who dwells among you, for you were strangers in the land of Egypt" (Leviticus 19:34, author's translation) to "you shall not strip your vineyard bare, or gather the fallen grapes of your vineyard; you shall leave them for the poor and the alien" (Leviticus 19:10) and "you shall not revile the deaf or put a stumbling block before the blind" (Leviticus 19:14). There are laws about how priests are to offer sacrifices, about how to plant fields, about the military and the monarchy, and so on.

These commandments have to be supplemented, since what works for a small group of people in a desert does not always make sense for people living in a large city under a monarchy, or in the Diaspora under foreign rule. Here is where groups like the Pharisees, who have what are called "the traditions of the elders" (see Mark 7:3-5; Matthew 15:3) come in; they sought to determine how best to enact the Torah. They would ask, for example, if we are to honor the sabbath and keep it holy, *how* do we do this? What should we do? What should we not do?

Society changes, and so laws change as well. Therefore, we in the United States have amendments to our Constitution. Similarly, church teachings change over time, for example, on questions of who can be ordained. And we always have to determine what are the weightier or more important commandments, the touchstones, and which are the lighter ones, which need to be interpreted in terms of those touchstones.

---

[*] Tradition holds that there are 248 limbs, or parts, of a human body (https://www.ou.org /torah/mitzvot/taryag/limbs/).

The Talmud, a collection of Jewish teaching compiled after the time of Jesus, provides a list that attempts to rank or, better, to summarize, the commandments. After Moses gave Israel 613 commandments, we read that David summarized the list with eleven. The reference is to Psalm 15, and the eleven include people "who stand by their oath even to their hurt; who do not lend money at interest, and do not take a bribe against the innocent" (Psalm 15:4-5). It's always a good exercise to determine, for each of us, what are the most important commandments. You might look at Psalm 15 to see what else this "Psalm of David" insists upon.

After David's distillation of the 613 into 11, the Talmud teaches that Isaiah 33:15 summarizes the Torah with six commandments: (1) "Those who walk righteously (2) and speak uprightly, (3) who despise the gain of oppression, (4) who wave away a bribe instead of accepting it, (5) who stop their ears from hearing of bloodshed and (6) shut their eyes from looking on evil." I particularly appreciate the concerns about stopping the ears and shutting the eyes. It is all too easy to ignore the cries of the hungry or the faces of the oppressed. When those television commercials about starving children appear, I am inclined to change the channel or hit the mute button. But I know that I am not doing what God wants me to do.

The prophet Micah (6:8) summarizes what God wishes for humanity with three commandments: "What does the LORD require of you but to do justice, and to love kindness, and to walk humbly with your God?" Isaiah 56:1 offers two commandments, "Thus says the LORD: Maintain justice, and do what is right, for soon my salvation will come, and my deliverance be revealed." Finally, the Talmud cites Habakkuk 2:4, "Look at the proud! Their spirit is not right in them, but the righteous live by their faith." This is the verse Paul cites in Romans 1:17 and Galatians 3:11, and the Epistle to the Hebrews 10:38 alludes to it as well.

This attempt to summarize tradition, practice, ethics, and morality all in a few lines is a salutary exercise. It does not mean that the laws and traditions that are not cited are to be ignored; it means that one model provides the guidance through which all other laws are to be interpreted. It may also be the case that one person's summary will differ from that of another (which is why the rabbis preserve all the different versions).

Thus, the scribe in Mark 12, who is impressed with Jesus' teaching, asks an earnest rather than snarky question, "Which commandment is the first of all?" (v. 28). Which is primary? Which should be the guide by which others are to be understood? The scribe wants to know.

Jesus provides him an answer that would have been familiar. He begins by citing Deuteronomy 6:4-5, "The first is, 'Hear, O Israel: the Lord our God, the Lord is one; you shall love the Lord your God with all your heart, and with all your soul, and with all your mind, and with all your strength'" (Mark 12: 29-30). This verse is part of Judaism's daily liturgy, and I cannot remember a time when I did not know these words. Yet when I read this verse in the Gospels, I was surprised to find the reference to "all your mind," because that is not in Deuteronomy. Jesus not only cites the verse, he *adds* to it. How Jewish! One takes a commandment, and then extends it to be sure that it is followed appropriately. In Judaism, this practice is known as "building a fence around the Law"; the practice helps us better follow what God wants us to do.

Then Jesus cites Leviticus 19:18, "You shall love your neighbor as yourself." We have seen these two verses put together earlier in the Gospel tradition. They are cited not by Jesus, but by the lawyer to whom Jesus will tell the famous parable of the good Samaritan.

The scribe is impressed. He acknowledges Jesus' response by repeating it and then concluding, "This is much more important than all whole burnt offerings and sacrifices" (Mark 12:33). Of course it is; no one would doubt that. There are greater commandments and lesser commandments. All are important, but some have greater weight than others.

For example, there's a commandment that says we are not supposed to work on the Sabbath. However, if our friend is having a heart attack, we call the ambulance, we perform CPR, we work to save a life. Jesus says the same thing: "Suppose one of you has only one sheep and it falls into a pit on the sabbath; will you not lay hold of it and lift it out? How much more valuable is a human being than a sheep! So it is lawful to do good on the sabbath" (Matthew 12:11-12). Therefore, Jesus would also heal on the Sabbath, because a person's life is even more important than a sheep. We are constantly prioritizing, and it is good to know what commandments help us in assessing priorities.

We are always juggling priorities. Occasionally, a student will ask me, "Can I get an extension on my paper?" I am not inclined to grant extensions (that would not be fair to the students who get their work in on time), so I ask, "Why do you need one?" If the response is, "I've got this other assignment due for church history class," I am inclined to say no. The New Testament paper is just as important as the church history paper (maybe even more so, but then again, I teach New Testament). But if the response is, "I've just been scheduled for an emergency C-section," of course the student gets the extension (and I'll likely knit her a baby blanket). Her pregnancy is more important than my term paper.

Jesus has cited two commandments, but he does not intend that one follows *only* those two commandments. Indeed, the other commandments show us *how* we love God and neighbor. And so we work our way back to Micah's 3, or Isaiah's 6, or David's 11, back to the 613 from Moses.

We should also work our way forward into the Gospels, because Jesus provides a *new* commandment. In John 13:34, he states, "I give you a new commandment, that you love one another. Just as I have loved you, you also should love one another." On first reading, this verse should sound peculiar. We've already read in Leviticus that we are to love our neighbors as ourselves and we are to love the stranger who dwells among us. The command to "love one another" is not new. Therefore, the focus of the verse must be on the second part, "as I have loved you." Jesus shows his love by willingly sacrificing his life. That's an extraordinary love, a love that risks all. But it is not an impossible love. Jesus is, once again, not asking anything of us that he does not ask of himself.

When we talk about loving God and loving neighbor, what do we mean by that? I love you, so I'll accept your invitation to dinner. Or, I love you, and I'll water your plants while you're on vacation. But what about, I love you, and I'll give my life for you?

The Love Commandment, together with the question of the Greatest Commandment, should also make us think about less drastic concerns. How much do we love God? Is our response, "Of course I love God, but I have a golf game on Sunday morning so I'll need to leave services early"? How much do we love one another? "Of course I love my friend, but I really don't have time to visit her in the hospital because I have a chapter on Jesus and health care due to my editor."

We should also see the Great Commandment, love of God and love of neighbor, infusing the rest of the Passion story. If we want to love God with our whole heart and soul, mind and might, we also need to think about how we deal with those moments when we do not feel God's love, when we, to quote the psalmist, "walk through the valley of the shadow of death" (Psalm 23:4 KJV). We realize that whatever love we may have for God, God's love for us is even stronger. Jesus again provides the model.

> **This love of God** means that we can be fully honest with God; we can say what is on our hearts and in our minds, no matter how painful those comments may be.

When Jesus prays in Gethsemane, "Let this cup pass from me" (Matthew 26:39), he is showing his tremendous love of God. He shows enough trust that he can say what he thinks. This love of God means that we can be fully honest with God; we can say what is on our hearts and in our minds, no matter how painful those comments may be. That is what Lament Psalms do; that is why Jesus, on the cross, cries out the first line of Psalm 22: "My God, my God, why have you forsaken me?" (Matthew 27:46; Mark 15:34). He knows that the psalm continues, "For he did not despise or abhor the affliction of the afflicted; he did not hide his face from me, but heard when I cried to him" (Psalm 22:24). The honest cry, the deep feeling of abandonment, is not the end of the psalm, or the story, or the good news.

The Lesson of the Widow's Mite

*He sat down opposite the treasury, and watched
the crowd putting money into the treasury. Many
rich people put in large sums. A poor widow came
and put in two small copper coins, which are
worth a penny. Then he called his disciples and
said to them, "Truly I tell you, this poor widow has
put in more than all those who are contributing to
the treasury. For all of them have contributed out
of their abundance; but she out of her poverty has
put in everything she had, all she had to live on."*

Mark 12:41-44 (see also Luke 21:1-4)

Our story is sometimes referred to as "the widow's mite." A
"mite" was the smallest copper coin used in England in 1611,
when the King James Version of the Bible was produced. The
Greek reads that the woman presented two *lepta*, the smallest
coin in circulation at the time of Jesus. Today, we might think of
the widow as offering not a grand silver denarius or a $100 check,
but two pennies, into the collection plate.

The title "widow's mite" is wrong for at least two reasons. First,
the story concerns two coins, not just one. Our widow could have
held one of those coins back, but she chose complete generosity.
Second, the story is *not* about the *money*, which is what the focus
on the "mite" suggests. We would not, I hope, refer to this story as
the "story about the two pennies." The story is about the *widow*,
impoverished, and yet willing to give all that she has.

To get to the deeper meaning of this short story, let's look first
at what the Greek actually says, and then, even more important,
we'll be able to see what, according to Mark, *Jesus* actually says.

There are several aspects about the NRSV's reading with which I would fuss, but two translations I find detract from the power of what Mark says. In the last line of the story, according to the NRSV, Jesus states, "Truly I tell you, this poor widow has put in more than all those who are contributing to the treasury. For all of them have contributed out of their abundance; but she out of her poverty has put in everything she had, all she had to live on." First, the word *truly* in Greek is "Amen"—yes, *amen*, the word most people say at the end of a prayer. Jesus on multiple occasions *begins* comments with "Amen" and even "Amen, amen." The NRSV nearly always gives this as "truly" or "very truly." "Amen" is a Hebrew term, which is connected to the word for "faith," and it might be better translated "so be it." Jeremiah 28:6 shows the ancient prophet using the same expression at the beginning of a sentence, to show the solemnity and import of his saying. If a sentence begins "amen" and ends with the concern that we *see* someone, we need to look, carefully.

Second, Jesus' comment does not speak of "all she had to live on." The Greek reads, "her whole life": Jesus' focus is not simply on her economic state; it is on her *life*. This is no small matter. It's everything she has.

Because we're in the Passion narrative, we know that Jesus will give his whole life. The widow, like Jesus, gives everything she has. She had two coins; she could have held one back. She doesn't. Jesus could have resisted the suffering. He doesn't. He could have resisted dying. He makes his decision to go to the cross.

Numerous sermons today regard the widow not as an exemplar but as a victim. They suggest the Temple personnel wanted to take every coin they could get. They compare the widow to the shut-in, on Social Security, who signs over her monthly check to the unscrupulous televangelist. Therefore, she is a victim if not a fool, and the money is going to line the pockets of a thief.

That's not what's going on here. Had Jesus thought exploitation was a problem, he would have called out, "Hey, lady, save your money." He's not incapable of disrupting Temple activities, as we have already seen.

Jesus is pointing out not exploitation, but generosity and trust. He compares her donation to that of others, "who have contributed out of their abundance." For a person with something to spare, giving a donation, even a tithe, is not going to create hardship. The widow gives everything.

On the other hand, the story prompts us to ask: "How has she come to this position?" What could we have done to prevent her from sinking into such poverty? Does she have children to support? Perhaps more difficult, has she been supporting a prodigal child who has taken his inheritance and spent it on drugs? Has she mismanaged the funds left to her by her husband, who had insisted on full control of the family estate and not allowed her to check the accounts? Was she misled by unscrupulous scribes who, as Jesus states, "devour widows' houses"? (Mark 12:40; Luke 20:47).

She is in the Temple, and we should see her there, for at least five reasons. First, and most prominent, she knows that this institution will provide for her, as it did for the prophet Anna, the widow whom we met earlier in the Temple in Luke 2:36. When congregants come to church on Easter Sunday, after they have spent time observing Lent, finding just the right tie, or just the right pair of shoes, do they consider those who might be in need?

Second, the Temple is a place—as the church should be— that welcomes both rich and poor. Yet there are a number of churches where a poor person, lacking the right clothes or the right zip code, would fear to step. More, there are a number of churches where formerly well-off people—whose investment failed, whose accounts are depleted because of medical bills, who have overextended—try to keep up appearances. They are among us, just hanging on, afraid to say anything. They need to know that the church will help them, support them, and not shame them.

Third, the Temple—as the church should be—is a place where all donations are of value. We might think of the member of the congregation who is on limited income. He too comes into the church, and he too puts what he has in the collection plate. We do not tell him, "Keep your money." That would humiliate him. Even the poorest of the poor have something to contribute. At the same time, we make sure that the money collected will be available to people who need the electric bill paid, transportation to get to work, or help with medical bills. Wholehearted donation has to be matched by wholehearted support.

A similar story appears in the Jewish source called *Leviticus Rabbah*, a commentary on the Book of Leviticus that dates to a few centuries after Jesus but preserves much earlier material. We read, "A woman once brought a handful of meal as an offering. The priest despised it. He said, 'What sort of offering is that? What is there in it for eating or for a sacrifice?' But in a dream it was said to the priest, 'Despise her not; but reckon it as if she had offered *herself* as a sacrifice'" (*Leviticus Rabbah* 3.5).

Fourth, we are reminded, if we *see* this widow as Jesus sees her, that the Jewish system does not blame poverty on sin. To the contrary, the Torah insists, repeatedly, that God is the special protector of the "poor, the widow, the orphan, and the stranger." Deuteronomy 15:11 states, "Since there will never cease to be some in need on the earth, I therefore command you, 'Open your hand to the poor and needy neighbor in your land.'"

Jesus will shortly cite the first line of this quotation to the people who grumble at the generosity of the woman who anoints him at dinner (Mark 14:7; Matthew 26:11). The poor are not to be honored *because* they are poor, as if being a widow or an orphan is a privilege. They are to be loved. I am reminded of the line, from the musical *Fiddler on the Roof*, when Tevye the milkman explains, "Oh Dear Lord, you made many, many poor people. I realize, of course, that it's no shame to be poor. But it's no great honor either!"

Finally, we must see this *widow*. I remember after my father died how some of my parents' friends stopped coming to the house, no longer invited my mother to dinner, no longer called. For some of these people, my mother was no longer a "friend" but a "fifth wheel." Do we see people who are widowed, or divorced— the single people in the congregation—and make them feel that they are fully welcome and fully valued?

As the church developed, the idea of giving everything to the poor and so becoming poor oneself became an ideal, but only for those who had the spiritual gift also to remain celibate. When a potential disciple, a young man who had it all but still felt spiritually empty, asked Jesus what he should do, Jesus instructed, "You lack one thing; go, sell what you own, and give the money to the poor, and you will have treasure in heaven; then come, follow me" (Mark 10:21). The young man, too stuffed by his stuff, too choked by the "cares of the world, and the lure of wealth, and the desire for other things" (Mark 4:19), cannot follow.

In the Temple, the widow makes a donation that, in the words of the scribe we just met, "is much more important than all whole burnt offerings and sacrifices" (Mark 12:33). Her two coins are worth more than the donation that allowed a new steeple to be built or the gift that allowed the coffee bar or the new silver candlesticks. She has "emptied herself," just as Jesus will do.

The widow's story asks what we think we should be doing with our money, and what we should be doing with our time. It also reminds us that how much trust we have in God is sometimes contingent on how much trust we have in the community, particularly the people who claim that they represent God.

Finally, Jesus asks his disciples to *see* the widow.

Do we see her and look away?

Do we count the amount she is donating?

Do we concern ourselves with where she will receive her next meal, and the one after that?

She does not speak; what might she say? And what might we need to hear?

Chapter 4

The First Dinner: Risking Rejection

Chapter 4

THE FIRST DINNER: RISKING REJECTION

While he was at Bethany in the house of Simon the leper, as he sat at the table, a woman came with an alabaster jar of very costly ointment of nard, and she broke open the jar and poured the ointment on his head. But some were there who said to one another in anger, "Why was the ointment wasted in this way? For this ointment could have been sold for more than three hundred denarii, and the money given to the poor." And they scolded her. But Jesus said, "Let her alone; why do you trouble her? She has performed a good service for me. For you always have the poor with you, and you can show kindness to them whenever you wish; but you will not always have me. She has done what she could; she has

*anointed my body beforehand for its burial. Truly
I tell you, wherever the good news is proclaimed
in the whole world, what she has done will be told
in remembrance of her."*

Mark 14:3-9 (see also Matthew 26:6-13)

*Six days before the Passover Jesus came to
Bethany, the home of Lazarus, whom he had
raised from the dead. There they gave a dinner for
him. Martha served, and Lazarus was one of those
at the table with him. Mary took a pound of costly
perfume made of pure nard, anointed Jesus' feet,
and wiped them with her hair. The house was
filled with the fragrance of the perfume. But Judas
Iscariot, one of his disciples (the one who was
about to betray him), said, "Why was this perfume
not sold for three hundred denarii and the money
given to the poor?" (He said this not because he
cared about the poor, but because he was a thief;
he kept the common purse and used to steal what
was put into it.) Jesus said, "Leave her alone. She
bought it so that she might keep it for the day of
my burial. You always have the poor with you, but
you do not always have me."*

John 12:1-8

Gathering for the "First Supper"

It would be nice if Lenten observances started with a "first supper," a celebration of the woman who anoints Jesus. Jesus states, "Truly [that is, "amen"] I tell you, wherever the good news is proclaimed in the whole world, what she has done will be told in remembrance of her" (Mark 14:9). Do we tell the story in her memory?

Perhaps we remember John's version of the story, where this "first supper" takes place at the home of Martha and Mary and their brother, Lazarus, whom Jesus raised from the dead. In Mark's story, the scene is set at the home of Simon the man who had suffered from leprosy.

Perhaps we remember, as John tells us, that it was Mary who anointed Jesus' feet. Mark, however, describes an unknown woman who anointed Jesus' head. Luke has a different story about a woman who anoints Jesus' feet—but this scene takes place not in that final week in Jerusalem but months before, and in Galilee. Luke 7:37 does not name the woman, but describes her as "a woman in the city, who was a sinner." In the next section in Luke's Gospel (8:1-3), we meet Mary Magdalene, "from whom seven demons [have] gone out" (v. 2). Over the centuries these various women have become conflated: Luke's woman who was a sinner *must* have been Mary Magdalene; Mary Magdalene therefore must be the sister of Martha who anointed Jesus' feet; the sin must have been prostitution, so Mary Magdalene must have been a prostitute; and so on. We conflate people and stories, and in doing so, we miss the distinct messages of each. The story is told, according to Mark, in memory of the unnamed woman—before we rush to name her, let us hear her own story as Mark tells us.

Perhaps we remember, as John recounts, that it was Judas who complained about the waste of the expensive ointment, not because he was concerned about the poor, but because he wanted the money for himself. In Mark's version, those who complain about the women's extravagant generosity are just some people sitting at table, and Matthew insists that the complainers were the "disciples." For Luke, Simon the Pharisee, the host of the dinner, complains (to himself) not about the woman's generosity but about her reputation as a sinner. Why does it matter *who* does the complaining? With whom do we identity? Just people at table, the disciples, a Pharisee, Judas? About what do we complain? How others choose to spend their money? Their motives? Their very presence?

What stories do we remember, and what do we do with our memories?

Let's start with Mark's cue: we have an unnamed woman, a woman who risks insult and humiliation by entering into a banquet and anointing Jesus. Let's look at her risk, and its rewards, and then at the other unnamed figures without whom the good news could not be fully proclaimed.

This first banquet is set in Bethany, which is also the home of Mary, Martha, and Lazarus (none of whom Mark or Matthew mentions). We are on the outskirts of Jerusalem and, unlike the Temple, we are in a home where Jesus can be at home among friends. He is not simply "seated" at the table; the Greek tells us that he is "reclining" at the table. In this scene, he would be lying on a couch, resting his head on his left hand, and eating with his right. No one seeks to test him, as did the Pharisees and the Herodians.

We do not know who Simon is. Perhaps he is the man whom Jesus cleansed from leprosy and commanded to make the offering that Moses set for recognition of this cleansing (see Mark 1:40/ Matthew 8:2). We might even think of this supper as being related to the Temple, where ritually pure people would come together to worship God and to eat the meat of the sacrifices.

The connection between the Temple and this First Supper— as well as the Last Supper—had already been anticipated in

Mark's Gospel. The events at the First Supper connect, over and over again, with the story of the poor widow whom he just met. Each story concerns a single woman, distinguished from among the more privileged people, who displays an extravagant gift. In each case she is silent, and in each case Jesus honors her by valuing her action. We are to see the first woman; we are to tell the story of the second. What again do we see, and what story do we tell?

We also need to assess her anointing before we can fully remember her story. There are different types of anointing. In New Testament studies, one of the first things students learn is that the word *christos*—whence we get the term "Christ"—means the "anointed one," and that it is a translation of the Hebrew term *mashiach*, which means "anointed one." However, the Bible (both Hebrew and Greek) has other terms that also mean "anoint," and it depicts various types of anointing. Kings such as David and Solomon and even Cyrus of Persia are anointed ones. Pillars and altars can be anointed, as can the ark of the covenant and, as we see in the Book of Ruth (3:3), women's bodies (the expression suggests putting on perfume). Corpses are anointed before they are buried. Our problem is therefore that when we read about someone or something being "anointed" in the Bible, we do not know if the underlying Hebrew or Greek concerns a commission sanctioned by God.

In Mark's story of the First Supper, the anointing is not associated with the term "*christos.*" When Jesus states, "she has anointed my body beforehand for its burial," he uses the Greek term "*myrizo,*" which means to have myrrh put on one's body. Her focus is not on divine commission or special calling; her focus is on the human body of Jesus.

Like the generous widow who gave "her whole life" to the Temple, our unnamed woman does something extraordinary. She enters a party, not at her house, and she anoints Jesus not on his feet, but on his head. And although Jesus says she has anointed him for his burial, the anointing scene is richer than that because anointing on the head is what one would do for a king. The word *christos* does not appear, but the action still retains this royal meaning to those who know, from other stories in Mark, that Jesus is the "son of David" and that he will die under the titulus "Jesus of Nazareth, King of the Jews."

This is an opening for us to talk not only about this one unnamed woman, but about all those women in the Gospels whose stories are not remembered and not told.

According to Jesus, she anoints him for his burial. But did *she* think that is what she was doing? Only our imagination can answer that question.

Jesus says, "Truly [Amen] I tell you, wherever the good news is proclaimed in the whole world, what she has done will be told in remembrance of her" (Mark 14:9). This is an opening for us to talk not only about this one unnamed woman, but about all those women in the Gospels whose stories are not remembered and not told.

The Women Who Followed Jesus

We could do another six-week study and more on these women. Along with our anointing woman, there are Anna the widow in the Temple, Mary Magdalene, the mother of James and John, Joanna and Susanna, Mary and Martha, the daughters of Jerusalem who weep for Jesus, the various women for whom Jesus grants a healing—Peter's mother-in-law, the Canaanite/Syro-Phoenician woman with her demon-possessed daughter, the widow of Nain whose son Jesus raises, the bent-over woman in the synagogue—the women who watch Jesus' crucifixion and come to his tomb to anoint him. . . . Each has her own story.

But we can fill in a few gaps about what their lives were like and what they risked to follow Jesus. For example, we know that women in Galilee and Judea owned their own property and had access to their own money. According to Luke 10:38, Martha welcomed Jesus into *her* house; that is, she is a homeowner. The house church in Jerusalem is at the home of Mary, the mother of John Mark (Acts 12:12). The woman who put her coins into the Temple treasury had access to her own funds, no matter how great or how limited. The woman who anoints Jesus has access to enough funds to buy perfume that could have supported a family for approximately a year.

There is no reason to assume that any of these women, including the anointing woman in Luke's version of this story, earned their income through prostitution; women could have been given gifts of money by family members; they could have earned money through textile work, pottery, wet-nursing, healing, cooking and cleaning, hair-dressing, even investing. Luke tells us that Mary Magdalene, Joanna the wife of Herod Antipas's manager, an otherwise unknown woman named Susanna, and many others served as patrons of Jesus' movement (see Luke 8:2-3).

These women also had freedom of travel: Mary visits her cousin Elizabeth; women travel with Jesus from Galilee to Jerusalem where we see them at Jesus' cross and then at his tomb.

They followed Jesus *not* because they were seeking freedom from some sort of repressive Jewish system that devalued them; they followed Jesus because he spoke to their heart and healed their bodies, and they found peace in his presence. It may be that many of the women who followed him also did so because he provided them a family that they otherwise lacked: most of the women named in the Gospels are not connected to husbands or fathers. They may have found compelling the story they heard about Jesus: He was sitting in a home and received the word that his mother and brothers and sisters are looking for him. But "looking at those who sat around him, he said, 'Here are my mother and my brothers! Whoever does the will of God is my brother and sister and mother'" (Mark 3:34-35). Yet Jesus also speaks of coming to bring a sword that will separate families and, following Micah 7:6, explicitly mentions women: "For I have come to set a man against his father, and a daughter against her mother, and a daughter-in-law against her mother-in-law" (Matthew 10:35). For women to follow Jesus, then and now, can mean a break from families—the daughter who worships in a different church from her mother or the daughter-in-law who leads her husband from one denomination to another. Yet all are in what Paul calls "the body of Christ" and so all are called to reconciliation.

> **They followed Jesus** because he spoke to their heart and healed their bodies, and they found peace in his presence.

The New York Times began in 2018 to run obituaries of women who have made remarkable contributions to history, politics, and culture. Their obituaries originally did not run in the *Times*, yet their stories are just as extraordinary as the ones that did appear. "Obituary writing is more about life than death: the last word, a testament to a human contribution," the series begins. "Yet who gets remembered—and how—inherently involves judgment."*

When we tell the story of the Passion, do we remember to tell the story of the anointing woman whose identity has been lost? Jesus himself calls for her remembrance. He is telling us that when we tell *his* story, we must tell her story as well. And today, when the stories are told, *we* are the ones telling the stories. And more, those stories need to do more than convey information: they should motivate and inspire, console and provide courage.

The Woman—or Women—Who Anoint

Matthew and Mark basically tell us the same story about an unnamed woman who anoints Jesus' head at the beginning of Passion Week; John names the woman as Mary the sister of Martha, and in John's account, Mary anoints Jesus' feet. Luke is the outlier, because Luke depicts the anointing as coming before Jesus starts to move to Jerusalem. In Luke, the setting is also at the home of a fellow named Simon, but this one is a Pharisee rather than a man cleansed from leprosy. The anointing woman, identified by Luke as a sinner from the city, anoints Jesus' feet. This narrative is not about anointing him for his burial and not for his kingship, but honoring him and showing her gratitude to him.

Jesus asks Simon the Pharisee, "Do you *see* this woman? (Luke 7:44, emphasis added), and we already know what happens

---

* Amisha Padnani and Jessica Bennett, "Overlooked," *The New York Times*, March 8, 2018.

in the Temple, when Jesus "also *saw* a poor widow" (Luke 21:2, emphasis added). Luke's anointing woman provides the occasion for Jesus to give a lesson about forgiveness. But that is a different story for a different time. Today, we are concentrating on the two versions of the anointing event that are part of the Passion narrative, the accounts in Mark and Matthew, and the account in John.

Mark tells us that a woman entered the dinner party. She was not a guest; she was not invited. She enters. The risk is already present: to walk into a gathering of strangers. It's scary enough in our world. Even to walk into a strange church, or a new Bible study, is frightening: Will I be judged? Will I be welcomed? Will I find a home?

She then takes another risk: she brings an *alabastron*, a vial containing "very costly ointment of nard"; we might think of very expensive perfume. She breaks the top of the vial, and she pours the ointment on Jesus' head. The risks continue as the people at the table begin to complain. We know what that's like. We've seen the looks of judgment, the silent attempts to shame us before anything is said. The people at the table began to say that the nard "could have been sold for more than three hundred denarii [enough to feed a family for approximately a year] and the money given to the poor" (Mark 14:5). They condemn her.

Who are these dinner guests to judge? Recently I was talking to a friend who in a moment of feeling guilty, took $100 and gave it to a homeless man on the street. My first reaction was, "Why did you give the money to him? Why didn't you give the money to a shelter where the homeless guy could go? Do you know what that homeless guy is going to do with that money?" I was assuming that the homeless man was going to get alcohol or get drugs. And then I realized: Who am I to judge? Who am I to judge my friend, and who am I to judge the man to whom she gave the money? And so I thought about Jesus, the woman, and the people who condemned her action. We have a moral question, and if the Gospels can open up moral questions like that, then they're doing their job.

The woman does not speak, but Jesus does. He responds by asserting, "Let her alone; why do you trouble her? She has performed a good service for me" (Mark 14:6). And he tells us that we need to come to the defense of our friends. If we have power, we need to use it for good, and that good entails speaking up on behalf of others.

He then alludes to Deuteronomy 15:11: "You will always have the poor with you." The NRSV translates the verse as "There will never cease to be some in need on the earth." The point is not that we should ignore the poor, or that we should despair because we can do nothing about solving the problem of poverty. The point is that we always have the opportunity to provide for others. Deuteronomy continues: "I therefore command you, 'Open your hand to the poor and needy neighbor in your land.'" It is our requirement, our mandate, to care for those for whom God cares.

This concern for the poor continues throughout the Old Testament. In 1 Samuel 2:7-8, Hannah sings, "The LORD makes poor and makes rich.... He raises up the poor from the dust; he lifts the needy from the ash heap." Ezekiel 16:49 explains the destruction of Sodom: "She and her daughters had pride, excess of food, and prosperous ease, but did not aid the poor and needy."

On occasion, I have heard people cite 2 Thessalonians 3:10, Paul's comment, "For even when we were with you, we gave you this command: Anyone unwilling to work should not eat." This verse has been used by politicians interested in cutting food stamps. But that is not what Paul is getting at. He is not talking about people who are lazy, who are refusing to work and living off the labor of others. He is most likely talking about those in the assembly—fellow followers of Jesus—who have stopped regular labor because they are convinced, based on a misunderstanding of Paul's teaching, that there is no longer any reason to work because Jesus is coming back soon.

Jesus, like his fellow Jews, would *of course* have expected people to help support the poor. But in *this* case, there is the need to support him. Following his allusion to Deuteronomy, he continues, "but you will not always have me. She has done what she could; she has anointed my body beforehand for its burial" (Mark 14:7-8). We give our resources, in generosity, even if they may seem wasteful. Bringing flowers to a friend in the hospital could be seen as waste: the flowers are just going to die, and there are poor people who could have used the money spent on the roses or the vase. But at that time, and in that place, the flowers can brighten the spirit of the one who is suffering.

A few years ago, a good friend of mine bought me a massage: I didn't ask for it; I thought it was indulgent; I had an article to finish. But she told me the money had already been spent, and that even if I did not want to go for me, I should go for her. So I went. It was one of the best things I have ever done. On that day, at that time, she knew what I needed, even more than I knew myself. Her generosity revived me. We need to care for our friends, and to do good things for them. The point is not to buy a bottle of Chanel every week; it is to know when, and where, and with what.

Ecclesiastes 3:4 tells us that there is a time to weep, and a time to laugh. A digression: Funny things happen when we mishear something. When I was in graduate school at Duke, my first year I was one of the anonymous graders for the undergraduate New Testament Intro class. We graders did not attend the lectures, but we were supposed to know the biblical text well enough to provide substantive comments on student exams. One exam asked about Mark's anointing woman. The professor wanted the students to explain what the woman did, how the people at table reacted, and what Jesus said. We know from the story that the woman anoints Jesus with nard, which is in the myrrh family. The problem: one student, who did not know what nard was, misheard the professor say not "nard" but "lard." Nor did he bother to read the Gospel. Therefore, he wrote on the exam that the woman anointed Jesus with lard, but since lard is a pork product, people complained. Then he concluded that Jesus announced that the woman had done a good thing, because he declared all food clean. So very wrong. Always read the Bible. Always check to make sure that what we have heard is what the text says.

When the text does not, however, provide us sufficient information, we can only speculate. We know almost nothing about this anointing woman: Did she spend her last denarius on the ointment, or did she have more at home? Did she seek to anoint Jesus as a king—because that is what anointing on the head can signal—or did she hear his predictions and know that he would suffer and die? Or was she simply trying to do something nice for him? Here we remember the famous words attributed to King David, "Thou anointest my head with oil; my cup runneth over" (Psalm 23:5b KJV).

Jesus says that she anointed him for his burial. If so, then she was the only one who took seriously his predictions that he would die. An unnamed woman, an outsider, understood part of the gospel message better than did Jesus' own disciples. Ironically, Mark will tell us that three named women—Mary Magdalene, Mary the mother of James, and Salome—"bought spices, so that they might go and anoint him" (Mark 16:1). They are too late: he has already been anointed, by this unnamed woman. Nor on that Easter Sunday do they need to anoint the corpse, for he has been raised from the dead.

Similarly, there are three named disciples who do not understand Jesus. In Gethsemane, Peter, James, and John fail Jesus. They fall asleep when he asks them to stay awake. At his arrest, they and the other disciples "all . . . deserted him and fled" (Mark 14:50). But another unnamed figure, another outsider, the Roman centurion at the cross, is the one who says, "Truly this man was God's Son!" (Mark 15:39).

Do we know the names of people who seek the same things we do? Might we learn from an outsider? And in some cases, might we risk being the outsider who can do what those on the inside can't, or won't?

Mary Took a Pound of Costly Perfume . . .

In Matthew and Mark, an unnamed woman anoints Jesus' head, for his burial, at the beginning of that last week in Jerusalem. People (in Mark) or the disciples (in Matthew) complain about the waste; they are concerned about the poor. In Luke, an unnamed woman from the city, a woman Luke calls a "sinner," anoints Jesus' feet. A Pharisee named Simon, in interior monologue, complains *about Jesus*, because he is allowing a woman who is a sinner to provide him a service. According to John, it is Mary the sister of Martha who anoints Jesus' feet at her own home, and it is Judas who complains, not because he cared about the poor, but because he wanted the money.

We might think of these four accounts as variations on a theme (anyone who has ever been through variations of "Twinkle, Twinkle, Little Star" will understand this allusion immediately).

All the variants are "correct" in that each one has the same basic structure, and all are different. The Gospel writers sing the good news with their own rhythms, and we should appreciate them all.

In John's version, we learn that after Mary anointed Jesus' feet, "the house was filled with the fragrance of the perfume." The observation contrasts with what we encountered— what we smelled—in the previous chapter. When Jesus was about to raise Lazarus from the dead, Mary's sister, Martha, exclaimed, "Lord, already there is a stench because he has been dead four days" (John 11:39). John wants us to experience the Gospel viscerally; not only by reading the words, but with sight and sound, smell and taste. The good news should impact all our senses, so that the world we encounter in its light, its sound, and its taste, is transformed.

Do we know the names of people who seek the same things we do? Might we learn from an outsider? And in some cases, might we risk being the outsider who can do what those on the inside can't, or won't?

Breathe in, and you can feel that "breath of life" known already from the garden of Eden. Taste the bread, and remember that John has told us that Jesus is the bread of life. Taste the grape, and remember that John has told us that Jesus is the true vine. See the sunshine, or even flip the switch in the bathroom, and remember that John has told us that Jesus is the light of the world. Touch the palm of your hand, and then touch the hand of your neighbor, and remember that John has told us that the word became flesh. And listen for the good news.

A woman anointed Jesus—who, where, when, why, and to what result? Each time we tell the story, the details may change. And that's okay. What story do we tell? How do we tell the story? And what do we proclaim not only in memory of Jesus but also "in memory of" that risk-taking woman?

Chapter 5

The Last Supper: Risking the Loss of Friends

Chapter 5

THE LAST SUPPER: RISKING THE LOSS OF FRIENDS

*When the hour came, he took his place at the
table, and the apostles with him. He said to them,
"I have eagerly desired to eat this Passover with
you before I suffer; for I tell you, I will not eat it
until it is fulfilled in the kingdom of God." Then
he took a cup, and after giving thanks he said,
"Take this and divide it among yourselves; for I
tell you that from now on I will not drink of the
fruit of the vine until the kingdom of God comes."
Then he took a loaf of bread, and when he had
given thanks, he broke it and gave it to them,
saying, "This is my body, which is given for you.
Do this in remembrance of me." And he did the
same with the cup after supper, saying, "This cup*

that is poured out for you is the new covenant in my blood. But see, the one who betrays me is with me, and his hand is on the table. For the Son of Man is going as it has been determined, but woe to that one by whom he is betrayed!" Then they began to ask one another which one of them it could be who would do this.

A dispute also arose among them as to which one of them was to be regarded as the greatest. But he said to them, "The kings of the Gentiles lord it over them; and those in authority over them are called benefactors. But not so with you; rather the greatest among you must become like the youngest, and the leader like one who serves. For who is greater, the one who is at the table or the one who serves? Is it not the one at the table? But I am among you as one who serves."

Luke 22:14-27

Now before the festival of the Passover, Jesus knew that his hour had come to depart from this world and go to the Father. Having loved his own who were in the world, he loved them to the end. The devil had already put it into the heart of Judas son of Simon Iscariot to betray him. And during supper Jesus, knowing that the Father had given all things into his hands, and that he had come from God and was going to God, got up from the table, took off his outer robe, and tied a towel around himself. Then he poured water into

*a basin and began to wash the disciples' feet and
to wipe them with the towel that was tied around
him. He came to Simon Peter, who said to him,
"Lord, are you going to wash my feet?" Jesus answered, "You do not know now what I am doing,
but later you will understand." Peter said to him,
"You will never wash my feet." Jesus answered,
"Unless I wash you, you have no share with me."
Simon Peter said to him, "Lord, not my feet only
but also my hands and my head!" Jesus said to
him, "One who has bathed does not need to wash,
except for the feet, but is entirely clean. And you
are clean, though not all of you." For he knew
who was to betray him; for this reason he said,
"Not all of you are clean."*

*After he had washed their feet, had put on his
robe, and had returned to the table, he said to
them, "Do you know what I have done to you? You
call me Teacher and Lord—and you are right, for
that is what I am. So if I, your Lord and Teacher,
have washed your feet, you also ought to wash
one another's feet. For I have set you an example,
that you also should do as I have done to you. Very
truly, I tell you, servants are not greater than their
master, nor are messengers greater than the one
who sent them."*

John 13:1-16

*For I received from the Lord what I also handed
on to you, that the Lord Jesus on the night when*

> he was betrayed took a loaf of bread, and when he
> had given thanks, he broke it and said, "This is my
> body that is for you. Do this in remembrance of
> me." In the same way he took the cup also, after
> supper, saying, "This cup is the new covenant
> in my blood. Do this, as often as you drink it, in
> remembrance of me." For as often as you eat this
> bread and drink the cup, you proclaim the Lord's
> death until he comes.
>
> 1 Corinthians 11:23-26

The four Evangelists give us four stories of the anointing woman, four variations on a theme. We have five variations for Jesus' Last Supper. The Synoptic Gospels—Matthew, Mark, and Luke—have the same emphases as does Paul: Jesus gives thanks, breaks the bread, distributes it, and tells his followers that the bread is his body. Then he takes the cup and proclaims it the covenant in his blood. But there are variations: Only Luke and Paul mention the "new covenant," only Luke places the dispute about greatness at the Last Supper, and so on. In John's Last Supper story Jesus does not speak of the bread and the wine as his body and blood; he had already done that in chapter 6, where following the feeding of the five thousand (the one miracle, aside from Jesus' own resurrection, that is in all four Gospels), he states, "Very truly, I tell you, unless you eat the flesh of the Son of Man and drink his blood, you have no life in you. Those who eat my flesh and drink my blood have eternal life, and I will raise them up on the last day; for my flesh is true food and my blood is true drink" (John 6:53-55).

Rather than rush to harmonize the accounts, we should savor each one. In this chapter, we'll look at several themes that the texts offer: the date of the Last Supper and its connection with the Passover meal called the *seder* (a Hebrew term meaning "order"), the betrayal, the bread and the cup, and the concern for service. As always, each text could have a chapter on its own; so could each verse. We can only give a foretaste, as it were, of the profound stories the Gospels and, here, Paul tell.

The Passover

For the Synoptic Gospels, but not for John, the Last Supper takes place on the first night of the Passover holiday. Paul doesn't give a date, but in 1 Corinthians 5:7-8, he does use Passover imagery. On that night, Jews celebrate the Passover with a meal called a seder, which commemorates the exodus from Egypt. We Jews will gather with friends and family members and retell the story of the Exodus. We eat special foods such as matzo (unleavened bread) to remind us of the unleavened bread the Israelite slaves ate in haste, since they did not have the time to allow the dough to rise. We eat bitter herbs such as horseradish to remind us of the bitterness of slavery. We dip green vegetables such as parsley or lettuce into salt water to remind us of the tears of the slaves. And we have four cups of wine, each with its own symbolic value. A piece of matzo is hidden, and the meal cannot be finished until it is found and eaten; hiding and then finding this hidden matzo keeps the children at the table awake, and the adults amused.

Some of the traditions, such as the unleavened bread and the bitter herbs, go back to the time of Jesus; many more were developed after the destruction of the Temple. Consequently, the Passover seder today is *not* the same as what Jesus and his followers would have done. And consequently as well, churches that celebrate a seder on Holy Thursday in the attempt to do what Jesus did at the Last Supper will not fully achieve their goal: they are not in Jerusalem; they are not eating lamb sacrificed at the Temple; most of the words recited at the seder were added after the destruction of the Temple; most of the foods eaten were not eaten in those ancient days (no matzo balls; no jelly candies); and so on.

And, just to clear up potential misunderstanding (since I've been asked about such matters): we Jews do not sacrifice animals (that stopped when the Temple was destroyed, two thousand years ago), and we do not put blood on our doorposts at Passover time.

At the time of Jesus, along with the unleavened bread and the bitter herbs, there were other Passover traditions that are no longer, and can no longer be, kept. At that time, one "ate the Passover," that is, the lamb, the Paschal offering, that had been sacrificed in the Temple that same day (the Jewish day begins at sundown, in accord with Genesis). That is why the Synoptics depict Jesus as telling his disciples, "Go and prepare the Passover meal for us that we may eat it" (Luke 22:8). At the Last Supper, as the Synoptic Gospels present it, the lamb sacrificed in the Temple would be part of the meal.

John has a different story to tell. For John, the Last Supper takes place twenty-four hours earlier, so that the meal is not a seder. In John's Gospel, Jesus is crucified not on the first day of the Passover, but the day before, when the lambs for the Passover seder are being sacrificed in the Temple. Thus, Jesus does not need to speak about eating the lamb, the Paschal offering, because in John's Gospel Jesus *is* the lamb. John has changed the symbolism. Whereas the Paschal offering, the lamb, is *not* a sin offering, John connects the images of lamb and sin-offering. We saw this as early as John 1, where John the Baptist says about

Jesus, "Here is the Lamb of God who takes away the sin of the world!" (1:29).

If we think of Jesus *as* the Passover offering, we can better understand how John's symbolism works. That first night of Passover, at the time of the exodus from Egypt, is when the angel of death "passed over" the houses of the Israelites, those houses marked with the blood of the original Paschal offering, but killed the firstborn of all the Egyptians (see Exodus 12:21-28). Jesus, as the new Paschal lamb, the lamb who takes away sin, will similarly save his people for eternal life. The original Passover marked the movement from slavery to freedom; the Passover for John, symbolically, marks the movement from sin to reconciliation, from death to life. Here we have another reason why churches that celebrate Passover seders might want to reconsider: if Jesus *is* the Passover, then celebrating a seder is unnecessary.

The original
Passover marked
the movement from
slavery to freedom;
the Passover for John,
symbolically, marks
the movement from sin
to reconciliation, from
death to life.

Betrayal

Paul's remembrance of Jesus' words opens with a translation problem. The NRSV reads, "on the night when he was betrayed" (1 Corinthians 11:23). This is a possible translation, but not the better one. The Greek term that the NRSV translates as "betrays" is *paradidomi*. It literally means to "hand over." In the rest of Paul's letters, nowhere does the apostle say anything about Jesus' being betrayed. To the contrary, when Paul uses the term *paradidomi* in relation to the cross, it is *always* God who "hands Jesus over" or "delivers Jesus" to death. For example, in Romans 8:32, Paul speaks of God, who "did not withhold his own Son, but gave him up [Greek: *paradidomi*] for all of us."

The term even functions as wordplay in 1 Corinthians 11:23, the very verse wherein Paul recounts the tradition of this meal. Literally, the Greek reads, "For I received from the Lord what I also handed over [from *paradidomi*] to you, that the Lord Jesus, on the night when he was handed over [from *paradidomi*], took bread." Not only does the Greek lack a reference to a "loaf," it also uses the same term, "handed over," twice. For Paul, there is no "betrayal," and so no need for a Judas.

Yet all four Gospels tell us that Judas betrayed Jesus, and all four Gospels locate Judas at the Last Supper. As we move from Mark to Matthew to Luke to John, Judas looks increasingly malevolent. It is therefore difficult to travel back behind the New Testament texts and find the "real" Judas. The Gospels leave us with different stories and so different impressions, each one worse than the previous one. Rather than debate the historicity of Judas, we do well to look at his individual stories, because here we can enter more deeply into the heart of the Passion narrative.

In Mark's account, Judas begins as an exemplary disciple: on the road with the other disciples, he heals, he exorcizes, he proclaims the good news. But immediately after that First Supper, when the woman anoints Jesus, Mark recounts, "Then Judas Iscariot, who was one of the twelve, went to the chief priests in order to betray him to them" (14:10). Mark gives Judas no motive. We could speculate that Judas was upset by the anointing, and the apparent waste, but all we have is speculation. Then, for Mark, the first words Jesus speaks at the Last Supper are, "Truly [Amen] I tell you, one of you will betray me, one who is eating with me" (Mark 14:18).

In Matthew's account, the timing following the First Supper is the same, but now Judas has a motive: greed. According to Matthew 26:15, Judas asks the high priests, "What will you give me if I betray him to you?" He receives the well-known "thirty pieces of silver" (the phrase does not appear in the other Gospels, but Matthew repeats it three times). Luke adds another detail: Judas is possessed. According to Luke 22:3, "Satan entered into Judas called Iscariot, who was one of the twelve." And John gives the story one more turn. Not only does John confirm Luke's point that "the devil had already put it into the heart of Judas son of Simon Iscariot to betray" Jesus (John 13:2), but we also learn that it was Judas, and not some unnamed person or disciple, who protested the anointing of Jesus, not because he was concerned for the poor, but because "he was a thief; he kept the common purse and used to steal what was put into it" (John 12:6).

Following the betrayal, Judas disappears from Mark's Gospel. In the Book of Acts, Luke tells us that Judas bought a field with the monies he gained from the betrayal; then, "falling headlong, he burst open in the middle and all his bowels gushed out" (Acts 1:18). Within a few years, the story became even more disgusting. Papias of Hierapolis, an early Church Father, reports that Judas had become so grotesque that he could no longer see, because his cheeks puffed up over his eyes (the rest of the account is even more outrageous). These are clearly cautionary tales: act like Judas, and you too will die in a disgraceful way.

Matthew tells a different story. In Matthew's account, Judas throws the pieces of silver back into the Temple and then hangs himself (Matthew 27:5). The story should remind us of Ahithophel, one of David's advisors. Ahithophel had affiliated himself with David's son Absalom, who was leading a civil war, and in that capacity, he attempted to betray David. When he realized that his plan would not succeed, "he set his house in order, and hanged himself" (2 Samuel 17:23). For Matthew, just as Ahithophel sought to betray David, so Judas betrayed the Son of David, and they both suffered the same fate.

We stop here to note the tragedy of suicide. The Bible never explicitly condemns suicide; it is never called an unforgivable sin. The suicides of Ahithophel and Judas are the acts of desperate people, people who believe they have failed their friends or their families, people who cannot live with the guilt of what they have done. And yet Judas was at the table with Jesus—he heard that Jesus would pour out his blood for his followers. Was he unable to believe there would still be a chance for him? What did the other eleven disciples say to him, or not say?

According to John, Jesus tells the disciples, "Did I not choose you, the twelve? Yet one of you is a devil" (John 6:70). He was speaking about Judas. In Matthew, Jesus states, "The Son of Man goes as it is written of him, but woe to that one by whom the Son of Man is betrayed! It would have been better for that one not to have been born" (Matthew 26:24). These are harsh sayings. It is our task, as readers of the Gospels, to determine what to make of them.

Since we will all most likely at some point in our lives be at table—at home, in an office, at church—with someone who has betrayed us, or perhaps someone whom we have betrayed, we need to remember not only the anointing woman who took risks, we need to remember Judas. In all four Gospels, Judas shares in the Last Supper. He is present in the Synoptics when Jesus speaks of his body and his blood, when Jesus distributes the bread, and when Jesus announces that he will be betrayed. Is Judas part of the group, or not? Has he a chance of being redeemed? Can he be saved?

Judas, too, is in the image and likeness of the divine. He is not a demon, although he may seem to us to be one. He is a human being. And we cannot afford to demonize human beings. Judas calls us to conscience.

Bread and Cup

Lent is often associated not with eating but with fasting—and in both cases we say something about who we are. It was the German philosopher Ludwig Feuerbach who said, "You are what you eat." Eating and fasting mark us as members of a particular community. Jews at the time of Jesus, as well as many Jews today, are distinguished by dietary practices: no blood, no shellfish, no pork products, and so on. Muslims too have dietary regulations. Some Christians will not consume blood, or meat that has not been properly butchered, in obedience to Acts 15:20, 29; 21:25. During Lent, some Christians will avoid eating certain foods that they happily consume the other days of the year. And many Christians are identified by participation in the Eucharist or Communion, whether daily, weekly, monthly, four times a year; whether with wafers or bread, whether with wine or grape juice. The details will differ congregation to congregation, but all the meals go back to this Last Supper.

When Jesus says, "Take; this is my body," and then lifts the cup and says, "This is my blood of the covenant, which is poured out for many" (Mark 14:22, 24), he is using sacrificial imagery. Today, sacrificial language does not resonate well with most of us, because we do not live in a culture where "sacrifice" in the sense of spilling blood on an altar and then eating part of the sacrificial offering is practiced. At the time of Jesus, everyone, whether Jewish or Samaritan or Gentile, understood the practice of, and the efficacy of, sacrifice.

Sacrifice was a way of sharing a meal with God, or if one were a pagan, the gods. It was a mechanism that bound families and communities together. And it had many functions, because there were many types of sacrifices: thanksgiving offerings, freewill offerings, dedicatory offerings, festal offerings, and yes, sin offerings. One could offer oil or grain or other agricultural produce, or an animal. Unless the sacrifice was what was called a "whole burnt offering," the worshiper would give the animal to the priest, and the priest would butcher it, drain the blood, burn parts of the offering on the altar, and give other parts back to the worshiper. In eating the meat, the worshiper would be, symbolically, sharing a meal with God.

But in no case, in the Jewish world, was blood to be eaten—not in the Temple, not in the home, not in the field. That commandment had been in place since the time of Noah, when God proclaimed, "you shall not eat flesh with its life, that is, its blood" (Genesis 9:4). (In Jewish practice to this day, those who keep the dietary regulations—and not all Jews do—blood remains forbidden. For example, if one cracks an egg and finds a bit of blood, the egg is not kosher and therefore cannot be eaten. Blood pudding—out of the question! Blood transfusions are, on the other hand, entirely permitted in Judaism, and donating blood is considered a *mitzvah,* a "good deed.") Nor is the eating of human flesh permitted, then or now. We can hear the shock of Jesus' words clearly in John's Gospel. Jesus says, "Unless you eat the flesh of the Son of Man and drink his blood, you have no life in you" (John 6:53). The disciples say, "This teaching is difficult; who can accept it?" (John 6:60). This is a good question.

It is essential that we hear the shock of the language. The shock is part of how Jesus teaches. He states, "If your eye causes you to stumble, tear it out; it is better for you to enter the kingdom of God with one eye than to have two eyes and to be thrown into hell" (Mark 9:47; see also Matthew 18:9). He states, "I say to you that if you are angry with a brother or sister, you will be liable to judgment; and if you insult a brother or sister, you will be liable to the council; and if you say, 'You fool,' you will be liable to the hell of fire" (Matthew 5:22). He states, "Love your enemies and pray for those who persecute you" (Matthew 5:44). These are hard sayings; we dare not dismiss them. But we must interpret them.

If we take the Eucharist for granted, if we take Communion as simply a form of dinner, then we miss the shock. Jesus is giving up his life, and he wants that to be remembered. He is allowing his body to be broken, and he wants that to be remembered. Paul takes this meal so seriously that he tells us in 1 Corinthians that whoever "eats the bread or drinks the cup of the Lord in an unworthy manner will be answerable for the body and blood of the Lord" and that those who "eat and drink without discerning the body, eat and drink judgment against themselves" (11:27, 29). By repeating the word *body*, Paul connects the body of Jesus with the body, and bodies, of those assembled in Jesus' name (12:12-31). If one eats and drinks but bears ill will against the neighbor, if one eats and drinks but has not been reconciled with other members of this body, then the body of the Christ—the church, and that which was offered for it—is profaned. Because some in Corinth did not appreciate the collective "body" of which they were members, "for this reason many of you are weak and ill, and some have died" (11:30). Participation in this meal is a joy, a blessing, a sign of life abundant . . . and a risk. The invitation to the table should come with a warning label: Am I reconciled to others in my world? If I am not, dare I approach?

We have already noted that Jesus says, "So when you are offering your gift at the altar, if you remember that your brother or sister has something against you, leave your gift there before the altar and go; first be reconciled to your brother or sister, and then come and offer your gift" (Matthew 5:23-24). He is not referring only to people who would offer a gift at the Jerusalem table; he is also likely alluding to the Cain and Abel story, where unreconciled issues that started with a gift at the altar eventually lead to murder. Jesus says, "Do this in remembrance of me"—I gave up my life. You need to respond.

Today, we talk about "breaking bread" together as a sign of peace, a sign of unity, or a sign of family. People still have family dinners, where on Sunday afternoons everyone shows up at Mom's house, or the Waffle House, or wherever the tradition dictates. When you participate in the Eucharist in a church context, everyone who is at that meal is at the same table with you. Instead of thinking of the front of the church as an altar, think about it as a table, and you are coming to the table of God. All of you are in the same family.

Service

Luke and John both connect the Last Supper with the call to service. In John's Gospel, the Last Supper also includes the scene of Jesus' washing the disciples' feet and his commanding them, "So if I, your Lord and Teacher, have washed your feet, you also ought to wash one another's feet. For I have set you an example, that you also should do as I have done to you" (John 13:14-15). Ironically, we had already seen a type of foot washing in John's Gospel, for in the previous chapter Mary, the sister of

Martha and Lazarus, "took a pound of costly perfume made of pure nard, anointed Jesus' feet, and wiped them with her hair" (John 12:3). There is also the scene in the Gospel of Luke when the woman from the city bathes Jesus' feet with her tears (Luke 7:36-50). I do wonder if Jesus took his cue from those anointing women, who provided a service to him. He does not always have to be original in order to be profound.

And profound John's teaching is. Foot washing takes on different symbolism depending upon whose feet are being washed and who is doing the washing. Foot washing—even more so than anointing with expensive perfume—is a sign of humility. It's a sign of service, and it is an action regularly in the first century performed by slaves. Jesus' point: no one is to lord it over another, and that those who claim to be his followers should do what he does, in service to others. Foot washing remains a liturgical tradition in some churches, where it is practiced on Maundy Thursday. (I admit that when I was a child, I thought this day was called "Monday Thursday" and always found that confusing. The increasingly popular designation "Holy Thursday" precludes this misunderstanding.)

When Jesus washes the disciples' feet, Peter says, "You will never wash my feet" (John 13:8). Because Jesus is the master and Peter the disciple, the idea that the master would wash the disciples' feet turns the world topsy-turvy. Disciples should be washing the master's feet. But Jesus says, "Unless I wash you, you have no share with me" (13:8). And then Peter, who takes everything with remarkable literalism, says, "Lord, not my feet only but also my hands and my head!" (13:9). He doesn't get the point. He may be thinking that the issue is hygiene, or something, *anything*, other than to ask him to act as a slave. Peter doesn't recognize what Jesus is doing. He is showing what humility, what meekness, what true service, looks like.

Many Americans don't like accepting service from others. We get nervous when friends, let alone strangers, go out of their way to be helpful, especially if they act in a way that is not convenient, or pleasant, for them personally. But Jesus teaches us that we need to receive, with gratitude, gifts that are appropriate to the occasion and marked by generosity. We have already seen that teaching in the story of the anointing woman. Then Jesus teaches us something more important: we need to be the ones who give as well. He came not to be served but to serve, and we should do the same thing (Matthew 20:28: "the Son of Man came not to be served but to serve, and to give his life a ransom for many").

Service is up close and personal; service is something others can see and appreciate; service means getting down off one's high horse and manifesting meekness and humility.

More, this type of service involves intimacy. Jesus is not suggesting we serve simply by writing a check, or even by stocking a food pantry. As the women who anointed his feet made direct physical contact with him, so he wants his disciples to make direct physical contact with others. Service is up close and personal; service is something others can see and appreciate; service means getting down off one's high horse and manifesting meekness and humility. It teaches us that we are not the important ones: the ones we serve are the ones who are important. And we, in turn, might receive that same service when we need it. The foot washing may be a singular event, but its meaning should permeate one's life.

Jesus has been proclaiming servant leadership all the way through the Gospels. Jesus is, according to Christian confession, "lord." The Greek term translated "lord," *kyrios*, means both "lord" in the sense of God as well as "lord" as in "lords and ladies" or "lord of the manor." Jesus insists on distinguishing his lordship from that second, earthly meaning. He tells his disciples in Mark 10:42-43, "You know that among the Gentiles those whom they recognize as their rulers lord it over them, and their great ones are tyrants over them. But it is not so among you; but whoever wishes to become great among you must be your servant." (The Greek for "servant" is *diakonos*, where we get the term "deacon.") This idea of servant leadership was, I think, a hallmark of Jesus' teaching, and it certainly was a hallmark of his

Jesus has been proclaiming servant leadership all the way through the Gospels.

early followers. The First Epistle of Peter similarly states, "Do not lord it over those in your charge, but be examples to the flock" (1 Peter 5:3).

And then we come to another hard saying. Jesus continues by insisting that his followers are not simply to be servants: "whoever wishes to be first among you must be slave of all" (Mark 10:44).[*] The language of becoming a slave should jar, should shock. To talk about slavery today is also, necessarily, to talk about slavery in our own contexts, whether the ongoing effects of the history of slavery in the United States, or to contemporary slavery and its corollary, human trafficking.

The week of the Last Supper is Passover, the time when Jews celebrate *freedom from slavery*. The time should remind us all that slavery still exists, and that its effects still exist.

---

[*]   See also Matthew 20:25-26; Luke 22:25.

A number of my students and friends wrestle with the idea that we are to be "slaves" to others; the idea of willingly becoming a slave, and therefore thinking that there is something good about slavery, is unthinkable to them. Others find the language of being a slave to God liberating. David calls himself a "slave" of God,[*] and he is recognized as such in the famous Psalm 89:20 (author's translation), "I have found my slave, with my holy oil I have anointed him"; so does Elijah when he says, "your slave my father David" (1 Kings 8:26, author's translation);[**] Mary, in her Magnificat, says, "Behold the slave of the Lord" (Luke 1:38, author's translation).[***] Only free people call themselves "slaves"—the point is, however, that these free people all had a choice. They could choose to give up their freedom to God, who then becomes the only master they can ever have. If God is their master, then no earthly master, no earthly slavery, has true power.

The idea makes sense. But it should not cause us to celebrate slavery; it should rather force us to remember that there are people, then and now, who suffer in slavery, from the Israelites in ancient Egypt to the slaves who appear in the New Testament, where they are told to be obedient to their masters, to the slaves who exist throughout the world today. It is insufficient, Jesus tells us at the Last Supper, to take up the role of a slave when we know there are actual slaves, human beings treated by other human beings as property. To be a servant leader, to take on the role of a slave, also means to take on the role of freeing others—not only from sin but also from bondage.

The risks of sharing that cup and eating that bread are high. We give up personal authority; we serve others, we are to free others.

---

[*]   1 Samuel 23:10; Psalm 78:70; and so on; the NRSV has "servant."

[**]   The NRSV again has "servant."

[***]   Translations that read "handmaiden" soften the Greek.

Chapter 6

Gethsemane: Risking Temptation

Chapter 6

GETHSEMANE: RISKING TEMPTATION

They went to a place called Gethsemane; and he said to his disciples, "Sit here while I pray." He took with him Peter and James and John, and began to be distressed and agitated. And he said to them, "I am deeply grieved, even to death; remain here, and keep awake." And going a little farther, he threw himself on the ground and prayed that, if it were possible, the hour might pass from him. He said, "Abba, Father, for you all things are possible; remove this cup from me; yet, not what I want, but what you want." He came and found them sleeping; and he said to Peter, "Simon, are you asleep? Could you not keep awake one hour? Keep awake and pray that you may not come into the time of trial; the spirit indeed is willing, but the flesh is weak." And again he went away and prayed, saying the same words. And once more he came and found them sleeping, for their eyes were very heavy; and they did not know what to say to him. He came a third time and said to them, "Are you still sleeping and taking your rest? Enough! The hour has come; the Son of Man is betrayed into the hands of sinners. Get up, let us be going. See, my betrayer is at hand."

Immediately, while he was still speaking, Judas, one of the twelve, arrived; and with him there was a crowd with swords and clubs, from the chief priests, the scribes, and the elders. Now the betrayer had given them a sign, saying, "The one I will kiss is the man; arrest him and lead him away under guard." So when he came, he went up to him at once and said, "Rabbi!" and kissed him. Then they laid hands on him and arrested him. But one of those who stood near drew his sword and struck the slave of the high priest, cutting off his ear. Then Jesus said to them, "Have you come out with swords and clubs to arrest me as though I were a bandit? Day after day I was with you in the temple teaching, and you did not arrest me. But let the scriptures be fulfilled." All of them deserted him and fled.

A certain young man was following him, wearing nothing but a linen cloth. They caught hold of him, but he left the linen cloth and ran off naked.

Mark 14:32-52

*After Jesus had spoken these words, he went out
with his disciples across the Kidron valley to a
place where there was a garden, which he and his
disciples entered. Now Judas, who betrayed him,
also knew the place, because Jesus often met there
with his disciples. So Judas brought a detachment
of soldiers together with police from the chief
priests and the Pharisees, and they came there
with lanterns and torches and weapons. Then
Jesus, knowing all that was to happen to him,
came forward and asked them, "Whom are you
looking for?" They answered, "Jesus of Nazareth."
Jesus replied, "I am he." Judas, who betrayed
him, was standing with them. When Jesus said
to them, "I am he," they stepped back and fell to
the ground. Again he asked them, "Whom are you
looking for?" And they said, "Jesus of Nazareth."
Jesus answered, "I told you that I am he. So if you
are looking for me, let these men go." This was to
fulfill the word that he had spoken, "I did not lose
a single one of those whom you gave me." Then
Simon Peter, who had a sword, drew it, struck the
high priest's slave, and cut off his right ear. The
slave's name was Malchus. Jesus said to Peter, "Put
your sword back into its sheath. Am I not to drink
the cup that the Father has given me?"*

John 18:1-11

The Gospels again present variations on a theme. The word
Gethsemane (Aramaic for "oil press") appears only in Matthew
(26:36) and Mark (14:32). Luke tends not to use Aramaic terms,

and in the Third Gospel the scene is set on the Mount of Olives (Luke 22:39). John places Jesus "across the Kidron valley to a place where there was a garden" (18:1). When we combine all these depictions, we get the expression "garden of Gethsemane."

In Matthew, Mark, and Luke, Jesus suffers. In Mark's account, he prays, "Abba [Aramaic for "father," *not* "daddy"], Father, for you all things are possible; remove this cup from me; yet, not what I want, but what you want" (14:36). As he awaits the time when he must drink this cup, he finds his closest disciples—Peter, James, and John—unable to stay awake and watch with him. In Matthew (26:38) and Mark (14:34), he voices his agony: "I am deeply grieved, even to death." According to one ancient manuscript tradition, "in his anguish he prayed more earnestly, and his sweat became like great drops of blood falling down on the ground" (Luke 22:44).

Here we also see the importance of prayer, even when we know the answer will be no. We see also the importance of being able to pray for ourselves.

Here we also see the importance of prayer, even when we know the answer will be no. We see also the importance of being able to pray for ourselves. Some of my students have told me that they worry about personal prayers. They should be praying, they say, for those who need healing or comfort, for those who are lonely and afraid, but they should not be praying for themselves. That would be selfish.

Nonsense! Jesus teaches us that we can, when we feel the need, pray for ourselves. As a Jew, he already knew the importance of personal prayer. Psalm 22, "My God, my God, why have you forsaken me?" (v. 1) is a personal prayer. Psalm 23, "The LORD is my shepherd" (v. 1), is a personal prayer. Job cries out in despair, as does Jeremiah. We need personal prayer—to sustain us, to help us find courage, to lament. Jesus provides the example that in cases of extreme concern, of course, we pray for ourselves.

"I don't want to die" is a very good prayer. Who might pray words like this? Firefighters, police, members of the military, those who work with victims of infectious diseases. Every day they might say, "Let this cup pass away from me. I don't want to do this, but I know this is my vocation, I know this is what I have to do." We pray to let the cup pass. We pray, "Let your will be done." That's Gethsemane.

But there is another setting as we enter into the Passion—not Gethsemane, the place of agony, but "a garden," a place where Jesus, the new Adam in a new garden, manifests his power. In the Fourth Gospel, Jesus is not in agony; he is in control. There is no prayer for the cup to pass, for Jesus has spent the entire Gospel in anticipation of his being "lifted up." Jesus identifies himself three times as "I am he" (18:5, 6, 8), but the Greek is simply *ego eimi*, "I AM"—the name of God according to the Greek translation of Exodus 3:14—this is the scene of Moses and the burning bush. *Ego eimi* is a phrase Jesus has also used throughout the Gospel: "*I am* the bread of life" (6:35, 48, emphasis added); "*I am* the light of the world" (8:12, emphasis added); "*I am* the good shepherd" (10:11, emphasis added); "*I am* the resurrection and the life" (11:25, emphasis added); "*I am* the true vine" (15:1, emphasis added); "*I am* the way, and the truth, and the life" (14:6, emphasis added). That "I am" in the garden is a manifestation of Jesus' identity, and his power. And it will be in a garden, according to John's Gospel, where Mary Magdalene will meet her resurrected rabbi.

The Gospels give us a choice, which is a blessing. We can choose which depiction speaks most fully to our hearts: the man of sorrows or the triumphant conqueror. Different people will necessarily have different perceptions of Jesus, and of God.

The Risks

In the Synoptic accounts, Gethsemane is the biggest risk of all. Jesus is about to be arrested. Could he have stopped the arrest? Of course. Could he have run away? Of course. His disciples are armed, so he could have asked them to do something. In Matthew's version of this story, Jesus asks those arresting him, "Do you think that I cannot appeal to my Father, and he will at once send me more than twelve legions of angels?" (Matthew 26:53). He could have called, in effect, the cavalry to Calvary. The risk is knowing that he can save himself and *choosing* not to do so.

Jesus tells his followers to pray, "Lead us not into temptation" (Matthew 6:13 NIV). He does not ask of his followers anything he does not ask of himself. He was tempted by Satan at the beginning of his mission to use his miraculous powers for his own benefit. Satan tells him to turn stones into bread to ease his hunger; Jesus instead presents his body as bread for the world. Satan urges him to throw himself off the Temple so that the angels would catch him; Jesus instead allows his body to be broken on the cross. Satan urges him to turn his worship from good to evil, to worship Satan himself rather than God. And Jesus refuses again, for "it is written, 'Worship the Lord your God, and serve only him'" (Matthew 4:10; Luke 4:8). It will be Jesus himself who will receive the worship of his followers.

Again, we saw Jesus being tested, being tempted, in the Temple by those who wanted to alienate his followers or compromise his reputation. He reminds us of that fact now, when he tells those who would arrest him, "Day after day I was with you in the temple teaching, and you did not arrest me. But let the scriptures be fulfilled" (Mark 14:49; see also Matthew 26:55).

There is also a divine risk. Jesus prays, "Remove this cup from me" (Mark 14:36). Removing the cup is, of course, in God's power to do. God has to refrain from using that heavenly power to stop the arrest, stop the trials, stop the suffering, and stop the death of his son. Jesus will suffer, and God will suffer as well. The darkening clouds at the cross are divine pathos. The rending of the Temple veil represents not some form of new access to God, since God is everywhere and everyone always has access. Rather, it represents God's mourning, for in Judaism, the sign of mourning is to tear one's garment.

The disciples risk as well. In Gethsemane, Jesus says to the disciples, "Sit here while I pray," and he takes with him Peter and James and John (Mark 14:32). These are the men who have been with him since his time in Galilee. These are among the first called. Jesus is distressed, he's agitated. He pleads, "I am deeply grieved, even to death; remain here, and keep awake" (Mark 14:34). And they can't. They fail, and yet somehow, they are redeemed. What happens when a friend calls and says, "I'm in hospice, please come visit me?" and we just can't do it? We fear the hospice, we fear death, we fear failing our friend. And then we feel guilt. What now? How can we make up our failures, when our friend is dead? Lent asks us: What

Lent asks us:

What do we need to do? Not *should* or *could* but *need*? Who might be depending on us?

do we need to do? Not *should* or *could* but *need*? Who might be depending on us?

Any time we are in relationship, we are always risking something. Going through Lent, we face stories of risk, of tragedy, of loss . . . and of remarkable courage. And of second chances.

Nonviolence

According to both Mark and Matthew, when Jesus is arrested, "one of those who stood near drew his sword and struck the slave of the high priest, cutting off his ear. Then Jesus said to them, 'Have you come out with swords and clubs to arrest me as though I were a bandit?'" (Mark 14:48; Matthew 26:55). Matthew then adds, "Jesus said to him, 'Put your sword back into its place; for all who take the sword will perish by the sword'" (Matthew 26:52). Luke adds to this scene both by noting that Jesus healed the slave (a point only Luke makes) and also by having Jesus say, "No more of this!" (Luke 22:51). Finally, John points out that the name of the slave was Malchus, and the person who struck him was Peter. Jesus then tells his disciple, "Put your sword back into its sheath. Am I not to drink the cup that the Father has given me?" (John 18:11).

All these incidents, variations on the account of Jesus' arrest, speak to the matters of arms and of self-preservation. When do we fight back? Alternatively, when do we engage in nonviolent resistance such as turning the other cheek and so confronting the violence without losing our humanity? When, if ever, do we allow others to engage in violence on our behalf?

I sometimes hear, in discussions of gun control, friends citing Luke 22:36. As his final words at the Last Supper in Luke, right after predicting Peter's denial, Jesus tells his disciples, "But now, the one who has a purse must take it, and likewise a bag. And the one who has no sword must sell his cloak and buy one." Moreover, we have seen in all four Gospels that at Jesus' arrest, some of his followers are armed. And yet, the next line from Luke's Gospel is Jesus' explanation for the swords: "For I tell you, this scripture must be fulfilled in me, 'And he was counted among the lawless'; and indeed what is written about me is being fulfilled" (22:37). The scriptural reference is to Isaiah 53:12, one of the "suffering slave" or "suffering servant" passages (the NRSV translates Isaiah's verse as "he was numbered with the transgressors").

The disciples respond, "Lord, look, here are two swords" and Jesus replies, "It is enough" (Luke 22:38). Enough for what? Certainly, two swords were not enough to protect Jesus from arrest. Are the armed disciples to represent the "lawless" or the "transgressors," or are the outlaws the arresting party? Is the point to have two swords for defense, but not for attack? Was Jesus speaking metaphorically, for the disciples would not have been purchasing swords in the market on the first night of Passover? We do know that Jesus expected the arrest to happen, and we see the tradition develop in the direction of having Jesus heal the slave's ear. His focus is on peaceful restitution, not violent resistance.

Finally, Jesus also warns the follower who struck the slave of the priest, "Put your sword back into its place; for all who take the sword will perish by the sword" (Matthew 26:52). The point is not that one should never take up a sword, but it is a warning about the danger of violent attack.

The Epistle to the Ephesians has a lot to say about weapons, but only metaphorically: "Put on the whole armor of God, so that you may be able to stand against the wiles of the devil.... The belt of truth...the breastplate of righteousness...the shield of faith...the helmet of salvation, and the sword of the Spirit, which is the word of God" (Ephesians 6:11-17). The author is not talking about packing an Uzi.

Jesus has predicted his death, and the time to put into motion the road to the cross has begun. He does not want the disciples fighting for him, and he does not want others to be injured. He knows what he must do, and he will do so without violence.

People will debate gun control and nonviolence, and they will come up with different answers. As far as I can tell, Jesus advocated confronting violence with *nonviolent resistance* when it was needed: Turning the other cheek means facing the violence head-on (literally). And yet, if one picks up the sword, one may well die by it.

We might do more here, when we realize that Luke 22:51, which the NRSV translates as "no more of this" could also be translated "Permit this." Jesus has predicted his death, and the time to put into motion the road to the cross has begun. He does not want the disciples fighting for him, and he does not want others to be injured. He knows what he must do, and he will do so without violence.

That Naked Young Man

The naked young man, who flees not only from Gethsemane in Mark 14:52 but also disappears in all the other Gospels, which do not mention him, remains a major topic of debate in biblical studies. Some think he might be Mark himself (putting in an appearance in the Gospel much as Alfred Hitchcock always put in a cameo in his movies); others think he is meant to represent the original Joseph in the Book of Genesis, who flees naked when Potiphar's wife grabs his garment after failing to seduce him (I see the connections of garment, young man, and nudity, but can't fathom what the point would be of putting that Joseph in Gethsemane). Perhaps he is meant to anticipate the next "young man" in the Gospel, the one dressed in a white robe who greets the women at the empty tomb (Mark 16:5). Or perhaps he was a disciple of Jesus who was preparing for baptism, James the brother of Jesus, another disciple, or Lazarus....The list is endless.

Or perhaps he is Mark's reader—fearful, naked, risking arrest himself, about to face the death of Jesus, and unable to do anything about it. He remains a mystery, and into his mystery we move, step by step, to the cross. We too are vulnerable and fearful, we too have deserted, we too have failed to stop what cannot be stopped. Before we can be built up, Lent will strip us down, and in that rawness, that openness, we can begin to heal. Before we get to the resurrection, there will be suffering, and crucifixion, and death.

AFTERWORD

The Fourth Gospel tells us that "Jesus did many other signs in the presence of his disciples, which are not written in this book" (John 20:30). The same can be said for the other events of the Passion that this short study cannot cover. As we've seen, each Gospel has its own variation on the major themes: the Triumphal Entry, the Temple incident, the Temple teachings, the anointing woman, the Last Supper, and Gethsemane/the arrest. Each Gospel needs its own series.

There are also other aspects of the Passion where much more is needed. We miss many of Jesus' teachings, parables, and invectives, such as the parable of the wicked tenants and the parable of the sheep and the goats; the laborers in the vineyard, and the wise and foolish virgins. We miss what he says to the Jewish and Roman political authorities. We should look more closely at the role of Peter, for example, of Caiaphas the High Priest, and of Pontius Pilate. We should look at how the people of Jerusalem are portrayed, how the women act at the cross and the tomb; we should remember the centurion who stands at the foot of the cross, and the two brigands who are crucified at Jesus' right and left hands. Matthew gives us a glimpse of Pilate's wife, and John marks the presence of Annas, the father-in-law of the current high priest. We meet servants in the high priest's courtyard, members of the Sanhedrin, and Roman soldiers. In each Gospel, the same song is played with a distinct tune, to a distinct rhythm.

Every time we read the Passion narratives, we become musicians ourselves, for we will always hear the text in a new key. Each time we read the text, we bring our own new selves to it—experiences, emotions, expectations. The story is a never-ending repository of inspiration and question.

As we leave these chapters, a few reminders:

- Entering the Passion means risk-taking; it means facing our fears, our failures, and our faults, and addressing them. Whom have we betrayed? denied? condemned?
- Entering the Passion means asking questions rather than settling for what we have always been taught.
- Entering the Passion means taking seriously, really seriously, what it means to be in Communion, and so to participate in Communion/Eucharist/fellowship meals with others.
- Entering the Passion means seeing old stories in new ways, and so challenging, or reinforcing, or supplementing those earlier views.
- Entering the Passion should give us courage—courage to lament, to embrace righteous anger, to see the course to the end.

- And entering the Passion should give us comfort as well—the comfort of knowing that death is not the end of the story, and the comfort of knowing that the good news continues not just when people proclaim it, but when they enact it.